Making the Training Process Work

Continuing Management Education Series

Under the Advisory Editorship of Albert W. Schrader

Making the Training Process Work

DONALD F. MICHALAK

Michalak Training Associates, Inc.
Birmingham, Michigan

EDWIN G. YAGER

Consulting Associates, Inc.
Southfield, Michigan

Harper & Row, Publishers

New York   Hagerstown   Philadelphia   San Francisco   London

To Lee and Judy
who endured when it was difficult for them
and encouraged when it was difficult for us.

Sponsoring Editor: Laurie Ann Caplane
Senior Production Manager: Kewal K. Sharma
Compositor: Maryland Linotype Composition Co., Inc.
Printer and Binder: The Maple Press Company
Art Studio: Vantage Art Inc.

Library of Congress Cataloging in Publication Data
Michalak, Donald F.
    Making the training process work.
    (Continuing management education series)
    Includes index.
    1. Employees, Training of. 2. Job analysis.
I. Yager, Edwin G., joint author. II. Title.
III. Series.
HF5549.5.T7M5   658.31'243   78-17907
ISBN 0-06-044429-0

Contents

Preface

From the beginning of our careers we have accepted the challenge to make the training process work. We are both practitioners and trainers. We have endeavored to avoid the temptation to become educational theorists in favor of becoming educators and trainers. In this book we discuss our experiences working in retail, marketing, engineering, and industrial organizations as trainers and in hundreds of organizations as training consultants.

We have related our experiences and techniques for the benefit of those who are new to the training process and need a broad survey, of those experienced training practitioners who need to sharpen skills, or of the training practitioners who will use our models to organize a focus effort. Probably most of our readers will find value by forwarding this book to managers, who also would benefit through a better understanding of the training process.

The book is based on two major assumptions we have proven through our work as consultants. The first assumption is that the trainer is an agent of change and the employer who pays wages expects the trainer to change people and situations. If a person finds that changing people is contrary to his or her values or is difficult to accept, then this field is not for that person. The second assumption is that all training can and should be evaluated, and if it cannot (that is, if no changes result that are measurable), the trainer should review seriously his or her involvement.

In a sense, the reader will find three distinct threads running through our analyses and recommendations. The first thread is one of organizational analysis. Throughout the book, the topics of data, their use, misuse, power, and value are emphasized. Data are critical to needs analysis, to management commitment, and to understanding, evaluation, and value analysis.

The second thread is the need for a correlation between training and organizational development. Training of any type is an intervention. The organization will experience some change as a result of the training. The trainer must be concerned with the direction of that change, the benefits to the organization, and the implications for the trainees as individuals.

The third thread relates to the role of the trainer. Throughout all the steps of the training process, the trainer serves as an analyst, a writer, a presenter, a helper, a counselor, and an evaluator. All of these roles are critical, difficult, and require a particularly sensitive balance between organizational and individual needs.

The central theme of this book is training as a process, not an isolated activity, program, seminar, or class. As such it involves needs analysis, development of objectives, estimation of outcomes and changes, management commitment (as differentiated from management approval or involvement), program design, classroom technique, evaluation, and maintenance of behavior. The reader will be taken step by step through our ideas and experiences to *make the training process work.*

We are appreciative of all our clients who have been so supportive of our efforts, the details of which we relate in this book.

Especially we thank our many friends in training and development at Ford Motor Company who have played such a key role in shaping our values and experiences. We also thank Geary Rummler, Karen Brethower, and Jay Hall, who worked out so many of their concepts with us in our early years and who tremendously influenced our thinking about the reality and practicality of training and development. We are appreciative also of the support and encouragement of Al Schrader, who has been one of the strongest advocates of making the training process work over these many years.

Don Michalak
Ed Yager

Chapter 1
Introduction

The material in this book represents a collection of our thoughts and ideas on what a training and development professional ought to know. The ideas are based on our experience. The examples are drawn from our work with a wide variety of clients in industry, sales, service, government, and education. The majority of the work we do falls into the categories of interpersonal-skills training and assessment. Approximately 20 percent of our programs deal with technical-skills training. For this reason the material in this book will lean in the direction of the nontechnical or interpersonal skills. We want to emphasize, however, that the training process (as we define it) works with technical training as well as with management training.

One of the major problems we faced when starting to write this book was deciding on whether to focus our attention on the experienced or the inexperienced trainer. (Many trainers face the same problem in the classroom. Some people in the class have a great deal of experience and some have very little or none at all. If the trainer aims at the experienced participants, the new people will be lost. Conversely, the experienced participants will be bored by a program aimed at newcomers.) If we were conducting a training session, we would have less of a problem. We would use some of the interactive models discussed in Chapter 5 to draw upon the experience of the one group to help teach the other, and we would draw upon the naivete of the newcomers to help the experienced people reexamine the way they act on the job.

Since, however, we were not working with a "live" audience, we decided, after much discussion, to focus on the relatively new trainer. Our intent is to provide a conceptual base so that trainers, especially those who are transferred from a management position into a training position, will get an overview of what effective training is and also learn some specific techniques to help make the training process work for them.

Our bias is that training is an ongoing process, not just a program. It reaches far beyond the classroom. Professional trainers generally agree with our bias, but management personnel often think of training as something that happens in a classroom (usually with a movie, slide film, or lecture).

We are disappointed that training continues to be looked upon so narrowly. We believe that workshops, seminars, and programs are important, but they represent only one part of the training process. Unless all parts of the training process are considered, training will be at best useless and may even be damaging.

Too often the training department of an organization is not looked upon as making a contribution to the bottom line of that organization, whether that bottom line be profit or service. We believe that until trainers look upon their contribution in the same way engineers look upon their contribution to the organization's goals, training will always be just a "nice thing to do." And as long as managers look upon the trainer's role simply as an organizer of programs for new employees, there will be serious deficiencies in the quality of service that the trainer can provide.

Unfortunately, the trainer's performance often is measured by the quantity of programs held, the number of participants involved, or the number of training hours used rather than on the effectiveness of the training. The trainer in such an organization is not really required to help management solve problems because management does not look upon training as a resource for problem solving.

During the past few years there has been an increased awareness in the training profession that training has failed to meet its obligations to management. There has been an explosion in the knowledge and understanding of how people and organizations behave and why they behave as they do. Armed with these new insights, trainers are trying to move away from the historic role of conference leader toward the more valuable role of management consultant on organizational dynamics. Needless to say, the transition has been beset with all sorts of problems, and management has not been able, except in cases of unusually talented trainers, to understand or assist in this transition. Many in-house trainers are experiencing role conflict. At professional meetings, in the literature, and from colleagues, trainers are learning the skills necessary to make them capable consultants to management on people problems (as opposed to technical problems). On the job, however, they are not given the opportunity to use these newly acquired talents. In fact, when people problems of major proportions arise, trainers often find themselves on the outside looking in. If they are brought in at all, it is just to run another program.

RESPONSIBILITY OF TRAINING

Training refers to *any* organized effort at behavior change, not just skills training. An important question that has to be answered is who is responsible for bringing about this change. Too often we hear managers and trainers alike assuming that trainers have this responsibility. Sometimes in a spirit of newly found awareness a few will say, "Managers are responsible for training, of course." We disagree with both extremes. Managers are responsible for assuring that employees are trained in their jobs. Trainers should function as a resource to assist the managers in training their employees but should not assume the total responsibility for the training. We strongly believe that it is wrong for trainers, however noble their intentions, to force training on managers who do not recognize the need for it in their organizations.

Our advice to trainers is to resist trying to train everybody in the organization. Avoid distributing fancy brochures that advertise a series of seminars. Avoid getting top management to force people to attend programs. Find a manager who recognizes the need for training and apply the training process to the manager's problem. When you do an outstanding job for one manager, the word will spread that training can be a valuable resource. Eventually, other managers will be knocking on your door.

OVERVIEW OF THIS BOOK

The following are the steps of the training process as we see and discuss them in this book.

1. *A need for training is somehow identified.* This happens in a number of different ways. A manager may notice that production or sales are down or that scrap or returns are up. New people or new equipment are brought into the organization. There may be unexpected downtime that needs to be filled. Whatever the route, someone in the organization has said, "We need a training program."

There is not too much that can be said about Step 1 except to warn the unwary trainer that the manager who identifies a problem in the department is often talking about symptoms rather than causes. It would be foolhardy for the trainer to design, develop, and conduct a training program based only on the manager's perception of what is needed. To do this without first pinpointing the cause of the problem is analogous to a doctor administering streptomycin to a patient upon request, without even studying the symptoms and running tests, in order to find the cause of the problem and treat it. In the same way, the trainer must first identify the symptoms and then ask some questions and conduct some tests to identify the causes of the problems. Once these causes have been identified, the trainer can administer the solution.

2. *A needs analysis is conducted to identify the causes of the problem.* Chapter 2 describes the conceptual framework from which a trainer should work when doing a needs analysis. Basically this framework distinguishes "Can't Do" problems (lack of skill/ knowledge) from "Don't Do" problems (motivational).

Six different needs analysis techniques are described in sufficient detail so that even a new trainer would be able to identify the specific problems to be solved.

3. *A task analysis may be conducted.* When a training program focuses on teaching people how to do a single job or on how to operate a specific piece of equipment, a task analysis generally is required. Through interviews and observation the trainer identifies what is done, how it is done, and what a person needs to know to do these tasks. The specific steps required for an accurate task analysis are covered, and a format for organizing and writing the data is demonstrated. A simplified version of task analysis is described for those situations that do not require the complete version.

4. *Behavioral objectives are identified, and management commitment is obtained for these behavioral objectives.* A well-defined set of behavioral objectives can be used to obtain management commitment. A simplified procedure for writing behavioral objectives is described.

5. *A strategy to bring about these behavioral objectives (it may be a training or it may be a nontraining response) is designed and developed.* The traditional "teaching" model often is not the most effective way to promote learning among trainees. An adult learning model involves

Awareness: What am I doing/not doing now?

Choice: What are my alternatives? What do the experts say?

Analysis: How does my performance rate when it is compared to the model?

Conclusions: What have I learned about the subject and about myself?

Practice: How do I make the new skill/learning a part of me?

Transfer: How can I put the new skill/learning to use on my job?

Basic factors (e.g., sequencing, methodology, testing, face-validity) are discussed to provide a model for the trainer designing a program. A number of techniques that involve the participant in the learning process are described, and various content-input techniques are evaluated in terms of matching the program design to the expected outcomes.

6. *The response to the problem is implemented.* If the response is a training program, it is conducted.

Some of the "tricks of the trade" are described in Chapter 6. Guidelines for facilities and other physical factors are given. Techniques for making effective presentations and leading discussions are identified. Some do's and don't's for working with audiovisuals are presented. Finally, an insider's discussion of an often misused technique, team teaching, is given.

7. *A maintenance of behavior program is implemented.* This assures that the effects of the solution that have been applied are not lost once the participants return to the job.

Chapter 7 describes the conclusions and recommendations that have resulted from a recent study on maintenance-of-behavior activities in industry. Maintenance activities should be included in the training program. Also management should implement maintenance activities on the job. A number of examples of each type are explained.

8. *Evaluation is conducted to determine the results of the training effort.* The dearth of evaluation on training efforts in business and industry contributes heavily to training's reputation as just a "nice thing to do." Chapter 8 lists reasons why the trainer

must take the time to do some evaluations. Techniques for assuring validity, reliability, and usability are described. Evaluation at four levels (participant reaction, participant learning, behavior change on the job, results to the organization) is described.

9. *Finally, there are some finishing touches that round off the process.* Chapter 9 covers some of these. Among the topics discussed are preparing a training proposal, writing leader's guides, and working with consultants.

CHANGE AGENTS

The emerging role of the trainer, as we see it, is that of a change agent rather than of a program conductor. The change agent is the person in the organization who is responsible for acting as a catalyst in bringing about changes that have been identified as necessary in the organization. The trainer specifically works in those areas where the changes are necessitated by people problems.

The remaining chapters of this book describe the tools that the change agent—the trainer—can use to assist management in producing required changes in personnel or in the organization.

Additional Reading

At the end of each chapter there is a list of books that may be of interest to those who wish to read more extensively on the subject of the chapter. It is not our intent to identify all the useful books on each subject. If we do not mention your favorite, we do not mean to imply in any way that it is not useful reading. We have limited the list of books to those that we have used in our learning process.

1. *Training and Development Handbook,* New York: McGraw-Hill, 1967.
2. *On Teaching Adults: An Anthology,* Miller, M. W. (Ed.), Chicago: Center for Study of Liberal Education for Adults, 1960.
3. *Supervisory Training and Development,* Kirkpatrick, D. L., Reading, Mass.: Addison-Wesley, 1971.
4. *The Supervisor as Instructor,* Broadwell, M. M., Reading, Mass.: Addison-Wesley, 1968.

Chapter 2
Needs Analysis

In this chapter we will describe several techniques that can be used in the needs analysis phase of training. In order to focus the trainer's effort during the needs analysis, an overview model is necessary. The work done by Robert Mager[1] in California and Geary Rummler[2] in New York supplies such a model.

A NEEDS ANALYSIS MODEL

Figure 2.1 is our version of the combined ideas of these two innovators. When we conduct a needs analysis for the development of a training program or a total management development system we use this model as a guideline for asking questions in an interview, for structuring questions in a questionnaire, or for analyzing the results of our investigation. Let us examine each step of this model.

[1] Robert F. Mager and Peter Pipe, *Analyzing Performance Problems* (Belmont, Calif.: Fearon Publishers, Inc., 1970).
[2] Geary A. Rummler, Joseph P. Yaney, and Albert W. Schrader, eds., *Managing the Instructional Programming Effort* (Ann Arbor, Mich.: Bureau of Industrial Relations, University of Michigan, 1967).

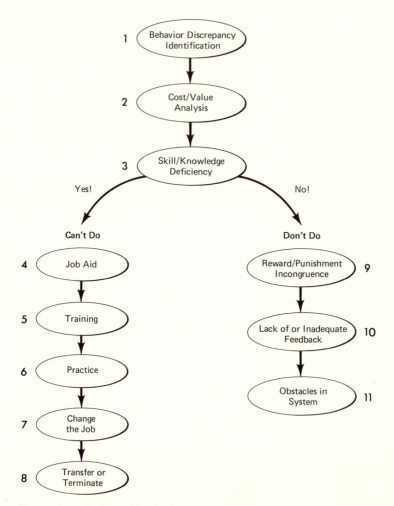

Figure 2.1   Training Needs Analysis Model

Item 1: Behavior Discrepancy Identification

The three words in Step 1 are all critical: "identify," "behavior," and "discrepancy." When managers look at a problem in their department often they do not *identify* the problem, but rather describe the symptoms, such as "high scrap rate," "low sales," "high absenteeism," and so on. The needs analysis must go beyond the symptoms. The causes must be identified.

The first word of item 1, "behavior," is perhaps the most important. When managers talk about a problem in their department, often they say something like, "My subordinates just do not have the right attitude." When managers say this, our response is,

"What are they doing that leads you to conclude they have bad attitudes?" The managers may respond with statements such as

"They don't talk to their people daily about housekeeping."

"Their scrap rate is running 10 percent higher than it ought to be."

"They allow employees to get away with infractions of the safety rules."

"They do not get their reports in on time."

These are performance factors, which as trainers we can work on.

The third word, "discrepancies," is subtly important. Sometimes the word "discrepancy" is replaced with "deficiency," but this is the wrong word. Notice the difference between managers' approaches to performance problems if they are thinking "deficiency" instead of "discrepancy." When managers think "deficiency," they have already made up their minds; that is, that the employees are not doing what they ought to be doing and are at fault. If, on the other hand, the managers think "discrepancy," then there is a possibility that when they analyze the performance problem, the managers will think, "The employees are not doing this the way I think it ought to be done. The problem may be in what they are doing or it may be in my expectations."

This analysis should give you information on identifying the problem to be solved. It also will provide you with the most important information you will need for later evaluation of your efforts; that is, this problem will be solved if your solution works. You will have specific information such as

"We expect our sales force to make 18 new contacts per week but we are averaging under 12."

"Our MBO reports are due in the first of the month but on the 10th of the month we are still nagging about one-quarter of the managers to get them in."

"We came out very poorly on the attitude survey we ran in the area of supervisor relations. Our employees feel that our supervisors are not giving them accurate information on the changes that are going on."

Item 2: Cost/Value Analysis

In many cases managers or supervisors have been promoted because of their technical proficiency rather than their managerial skills. These managers often think, "Employees ought to be doing things

the way I did them. It was successful for me. It will work for them."
That, of course, is not always true. When you discuss a potential
training program with a manager, you need to have the manager
confront the questions, "Is it important that this change be made?"
or, "Is this change just a personal whim?"

An example of a change that is not important will demonstrate
what we mean. Sometimes a manager wants the employees to write
the way he or she does. When the trainer looks at samples of the
employees' writing, often it is obvious that although the writing
styles could be improved somewhat, the writing itself is clear and
the message gets across. The manager should be questioned about
whether or not the cost of the training is really worth the results
that will be obtained. Is avoiding dangling participles or writing
more directly really going to improve the performance of the employees or does the training fall into the "nice to do" category?

Sometimes a more detailed analysis is necessary. A comparison
of the cost of the training versus the value of solving the problem
may help the manager decide whether or not to attack the problem.
A question that can provide valuable information is, "What is the
cost of *not* solving the problem?" If the cost of solving the problem
is too high, management may choose to live with the current situation. The object is to avoid those automatic decisions that are based
on personal whim and do not contribute to real organization
effectiveness.

Item 3: Skill/Knowledge Deficiency

We now come to the pivotal point of this model. The question to
be answered is, "Is this a skill/knowledge deficiency?"; that is, is
the performance discrepancy caused by something that the employees do not know or are not able to do? A tongue-in-cheek
question that can be asked is this: "If the employees' lives depended
on it, could they do it?"

For example, suppose you say to a salesclerk in a shoe store,
whose manager claims that the salesclerk does not suggestion sell,
"I have a loaded pistol here, and after you finish the sale with the
next five customers I want you to suggest another item—shoe polish,
socks, or shoelaces. Do you understand?" The salesclerk says, "Yes,"
and after the customer purchases shoes, the salesclerk suggests that
the customer may need polish, socks, or shoelaces. Under such stress
the salesclerk is able to do all that the manager wants and yet does
not perform—or does not perform consistently—on the job. We

call this a "Don't Do" problem, because although the salesclerk has the skills and knowledge to do the task, it does not get done for some reason (as yet unidentified). The potential solution to a "Don't Do" problem will be found in items 9–11 of this model (See Figure 2.1).

On the other hand, if after the customer buys a pair of brown shoes, the salesclerk suggests that perhaps the customer might want to buy a pair of *black* socks or *blue* shoe polish, we have an example of a skill or knowledge deficiency. Even though he or she knows life depends on making the suggestion, this salesclerk cannot perform. In this case, we say that the salesclerk has a "Can't Do" problem, and the solution to the problem will lie on the left side of the model.

"CAN'T DO" PROBLEMS

Let us study the left side of the model first, the "Can't Do" side. In "Can't Do" problems we are assuming that employees have skill or knowledge deficiencies; that is, there is something they do not know or are not able to do.

Item 4: Job Aid

One of the quickest and most effective methods for solving a "Can't Do" problem is giving the employee a job aid. This is especially true when there is a considerable amount of detail to be learned. Two examples will demonstrate what we mean.

A large warehouse operation changed from a multiform to a single-form system. A single computerized form was generated, which followed the shipment through the warehouse process. The form was so complicated that most of the workers in the warehouse were not able to deal with it properly. The training manager was asked to conduct a program on how to complete the form. Because different parts of the form had to be used at various stations in the warehouse and because there was a myriad of details to be remembered, mistakes were still being made after the training. In fact, month-old orders were found still on the tow motor cars traveling around the warehouse because the workers who had picked the order did not know what to do with the form.

The solution was a job aid. Each work station was given a clipboard that had a plastic flap. When the order came to the work station, the form was put into the clipboard and the plastic flap was laid over the order. There were holes in the plastic flap at the points where something had to be written or done. In addition, the instructions were written on the plastic flap: for example, "Count the number of boxes and insert that number here," or, "Read the address on the shipping label and if it is the same as the address here, check this box." There really was no need to train the workers. If they could read and write, they were able to handle the form perfectly with the job aid.

Other examples of a job aid are seen in complex assembly operations. In energy control systems for jet airplanes (which have 35,000 parts and are produced at a rate of one or two per month), it would be practically impossible for one person to remember the entire procedure, and it would not be economically feasible to try to train one person to do that. A system using slides, workbooks, and, in some cases, audio tapes was developed so that a trained technician, simply by following the process described in the sound/ slide and printed material, was able to assemble a very complex piece of equipment correctly.

Item 5: Training

When an employee lacks the skill or knowledge to do a job properly, training is usually seen as the solution. Even though we are in the business of conducting and designing training programs, we do not advocate training as the first or the best solution to performance problems. As a matter of fact, of all the solutions listed on the chart in Figure 2.2, training is sometimes the most expensive and the least effective solution. If training is the answer, however, this book will help you to ensure its effectiveness.

Item 6: Practice

When an employee loses the skill or knowledge in which he or she was once trained because the skill or knowledge has not been used often, the problem is a lack of practice. A classic example of this is seen in the airline industry. The one skill that every airline employee practices regularly is how to deal with an emergency situation. The airlines recognize (as does the FAA) that the odds are very high that a person trained in emergency procedures will never have the opportunity to use them and, consequently, will forget much of the detail. Practice sessions must be held regularly. (Law enforcement officers are faced with the same situation with

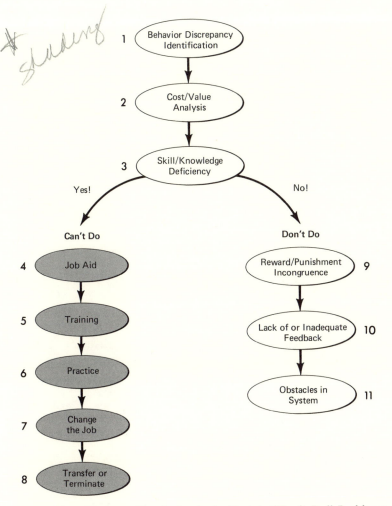

Figure 2.2   Training Needs Analysis Model: "Can't Do" Problems

weapons training. The vast majority of law enforcement officers seldom, if ever, fire their weapons and, thus, must return to the range for regular practice.)

Item 7: Change the Job

Usually, when a trainer or a manager looks at a performance discrepancy, the first thought is to change the employee. In some cases, however, if the job were changed, the employee might be able to perform. A simple example of this is when the employee cannot reach the equipment because he or she is too short. Rather than saying, "Let's get a taller employee," the problem could be approached from the point of view of changing the job. Can the equipment be lowered? Can the employee stand on a platform?

Sometimes a complex job can be changed by subdivision. The typical sales job, for example, consists of at least three parts: prospecting, demonstrating, and closing. Over the years sales managers have tried in vain to find and train salespeople to do all three steps. Their success ratio has, in general, been discouragingly low. A number of sales organizations, particularly in the automobile and the real estate industries, have found that some people are excellent at prospecting and demonstrating but not at closing. Rather than wasting time and money trying to train these people to be good closers, the organizations have found that they can subdivide the sales job: one person prospects and demonstrates and another closes. Many automobile dealerships and real estate agencies have increased their sales by subdividing jobs.

Item 8: Transfer or Terminate

Another solution to a performance discrepancy problem is to transfer the employee to an area in which that employee's skills and knowledge will be sufficient for the job. The ultimate solution is termination.

"DON'T DO" PROBLEMS

Now, let us look at the other side of the model, the "Don't Do" side. (See Figure 2.3.) We go to this side of the model if our analysis shows that the employee does have the skill or knowledge necessary to perform but is not performing properly. In these situations, all the training in the world will not help. It has been our experience that even without any training, many people could perform if the problems listed in items 9–11 on this model were eliminated.

Item 9: Reward/Punishment Incongruence

Sometimes from the employee's point of view, it is a punishment to perform the job the way management wishes. A common example of this is peer pressure on many hourly jobs. The new employee wants to do a good job and, in fact, exerts a little extra effort. In a short time the employee finds out from peers that "rate busters" are not appreciated. Since management never really commended

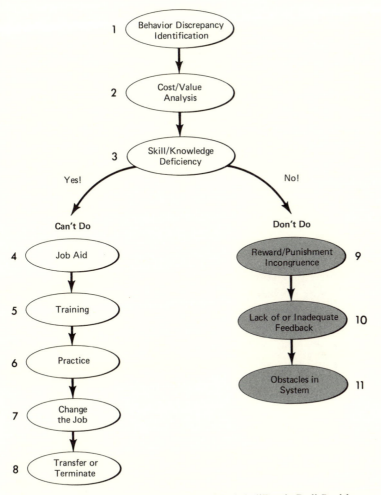

Figure 2.3   Training Needs Analysis Model: "Don't Do" Problems

the extra effort, the employee, not wanting to risk the alienation of peers, slides into mediocrity.

Another example of this is a performance review. Very often companies complain that managers do a poor job writing performance reviews. Their solution to this often is a training program on how to write performance appraisals. This seldom improves behavior because it is not a "Can't Do" problem; it is a "Don't Do" problem. In many organizations, a manager has to take the work home. There just is not enough time on the job to spend the two or three hours needed to write a good performance appraisal. Thus, performance is punishing. Managers have to give up some of their own time in order to do the job the way management wants it done.

Another factor is honesty in rating an employee. It is often punishing to the manager to rate the employee at a satisfactory level rather than a satisfactory-plus level if the lower rating eliminates the employee from the possibility of a merit increase for the succeeding year. Many managers in this circumstance will decide that it may be too damaging to their relationship with the employee to be completely honest and thus may hedge a little and rate the employee at satisfactory-plus. In this way they avoid the punishment of having to face the employee with a low rating.

A third example is the classic situation of the employee who works hard, only to be rewarded with more work. Sometimes, nonperformance is rewarding (i.e., not doing a job the way management wants it done is seen by the employee as rewarding). In the automobile sales business, for example, there is evidence to support the theory that if you can get the customer to drive the automobile, you have increased your chances of selling that car. And yet, in dealership after dealership, we find many salespeople who avoid giving a demonstration ride. When we interview these salespeople, they quote all sorts of negative stories: When they did try to conduct a demonstration ride, the car would not start, the car was dirty, the radio did not work properly, there was a squeak in the car, and so forth, and these things lost the sale (at least in the mind of the salesperson).

Other common examples are frequent absences because of a distasteful job or a disliked supervisor, working slowly enough to do one job instead of two in a day, working slowly in order to get overtime work, and so forth.

When you do a needs analysis in an organization and a manager reports that people are not performing the way they ought to be performing, you need to ask some questions that delve into the *real* reward system operating in the organization. Find out from the performer's point of view whether the performance is punishing or rewarding or whether not doing it at all has its own rewards.

Item 10: Lack of or Inadequate Feedback

The quickest way to change employees' behavior is to give them feedback that what they are doing or not doing, is not productive. Often employees say, "I just never knew that I was supposed to do it that way. I have been doing it this way ever since I started here and you are the first person to tell me that."

If you see that employees are not performing the way they should and after some investigation you find out they do have the skills and knowledge, perhaps the problem is a simple matter of feedback. An example will demonstrate this point. In a large retail store customers who want to charge a purchase but do not have their charge plate can do so if they present a driver's license. The salesclerks have been trained to print the sales ticket to assure that the proper charge is made. The vast majority of the salesclerks, however, are writing, not printing the sales tickets. For the first four or five days on the job the new salesclerk prints out the sales ticket, as learned in training. However, on Saturday there is a big sale and the store is crowded with customers. All the experienced salesclerks are working in order to cover the sale. While the new salesclerk is laboriously printing out a sales ticket, one of the experienced salesclerks approaches and says, "Watcha doin'?" The new salesclerk replies, "I'm printing the sales ticket as they taught me in training." The experienced clerk says, "Hey, we don't have time for that. Come on, let's get moving." Even though he or she does not feel good about it, the new salesclerk starts writing the sales ticket and because of the pressures received from peers, does so for the rest of the day but expects that come Monday morning, the supervisor is going to be upset. When Monday comes, the supervisor does not say anything at all. Being well trained, however, the new clerk goes back to printing the sales tickets. On Thursday, the big weekend sales start. Once again, under the pressure of clammering customers and peers the new clerk goes back to writing the sales tickets. Once again, on the following Monday, the supervisor says nothing. It soon becomes apparent that it really does not seem to make any difference if the sales tickets are written or printed.

When you interview a manager about a performance discrepancy in the organization, you need to find out what happens when the employees do a job correctly as well as incorrectly. Is there any feedback?

Item 11: Obstacles in the System

Obstacles probably are the most common reason that employees do not do things they know how to do. Here is a silly example: Someone hands you a clarinet and says, "I'll give you $1000 if you play 'Yankee Doodle.'" Assuming you know how to play a clarinet, you wet your lips, put the clarinet to your mouth, and then notice there is no reed in the clarinet. When you mention it, the person says, "Quit griping. Just play the song."

Managers often do this same kind of thing. They make demands of employees, but the system does not support the skills and knowledge they have. The most common obstacle is having too many tasks to perform and too little time in which to perform them. In one large manufacturing firm, the training manager was called in by top management to teach all the supervisors how to orient new employees. An excellent two-hour training program was developed, and every supervisor participated in the program. A few months later it was found that performance had not changed at all. The same slip-shod orientations were being conducted. Investigation showed that there were obstacles in the system. The most critical part of a first-line supervisor's job is the first hour. The supervisor does not know which employees have shown up, whether there are any parts shortages, or whether any of the equipment is down. If the supervisor makes the correct decisions, the rest of the day will run fairly smoothly. In addition to these decisions, the supervisor is expected to spend 20 minutes orienting the new employees to the job, but it just cannot be done. If the supervisor does take the time to do the orientation properly, other, more essential parts of the job would have to be skipped.

Another example of obstacles occurred in the shipping department of a large company. The shipping manager wanted us to develop a training program to teach the workers how to address the labels properly. After looking at the labels we recognized that anyone who could address an ordinary envelope could address one of the labels. We interviewed the shipping dock workers and found that mislabeling did not occur consistently throughout the month. It happened more often near the end of the month when there were time pressures. The company wanted to ship as much as possible at the end of the month so that it could bill its customers. The workers on the shipping dock, even though they knew the proper procedures, often violated them. For example, when a shipping invoice came down from accounting with the zip code missing, the shipping clerk ordinarily called upstairs or checked in the zip code manual to fill it in but near the end of the month made a guess at it.

The needs analysis model we have described in considerable detail provides direction for the trainer conducting a needs analysis. At the end of the needs analysis the trainer needs to know

what the discrepancies are in behavioral terms
whether changing the discrepancies is important
whether the performance discrepancies are the result of a lack
 of skill or knowledge on the part of the performer ("Can't

Do"); if they are, the left side of the model is followed to identify the most effective and least costly solution

You need answers to the questions on the right side of the model if the performance discrepancy is not a skill or knowledge deficiency, but is a "Don't Do" problem.

WHY USE NEEDS ANALYSIS TECHNIQUES

There are four major reasons why a needs analysis must be done before the training program is developed.

1. *Identify specific problem areas in the organization.* The first and most important reason for using needs analysis techniques is that both the trainer and management will know the problems of the organization so that the most appropriate training response (if there should be a training response) will be directed to those organizational problems. If a manager approaches the training department with a request for a communications program, for example, too many trainers (in their exuberance to serve management) will scout around to find a good communications program and conduct the training. Our experience is that this approach almost inevitably is doomed to failure. The people will leave the training program nodding their heads appreciatively, saying, "That was a good program," but when they go back to their organizations business will proceed as usual because the training was not directed to the real needs of the participants.

A better response to the request for a communications training program would be to say, "Yes, let's start by taking a look at the situation; we will talk to a few people to find the problems so that when we develop the program, we can zero in on your situation rather than just use a shotgun approach."

2. *Obtain management commitment.* The common management opinion of training as a "nice thing to do" can be laid directly at the doorstep of poor or nonexistent needs analysis. The way to obtain management commitment to training is to make sure that the training directly affects what happens in that manager's organization. Trainers should see themselves in the same way that controllers or engineering managers see their departments, that is, as making direct contributions to the bottom line.

Trainers must be careful so that they do not kid themselves into thinking management commitment is present because managers approve of, support, pay for, send people to, or even help teach in the training program. Management commitment comes from the knowledge that the training will affect performance, profit, results, and, thus, their own performance. At the end of the year all managers must account for themselves. If training clearly improves their performance—and they will know it—then trainers will always have true management commitment. It has been our experience that when a trainer can improve the productivity of the manager's human resources and thereby improve performance on the job, management commitment follows. Training programs will be supported by management rather than avoided or cut by them; training budgets will be supported by management rather than trimmed. The problem of taking employees off the job and putting them into a classroom will become less the trainer's problem than a co-problem of management and trainer.

3. *Develop "before" data for effective evaluation.* Another very important reason for doing a needs analysis is that unless some data are developed prior to the training program, the evaluations that take place after the program is completed may not be valid. By looking at the data before any training is done the trainer can establish milestones against which to measure the effectiveness of the training conducted. We will talk much more extensively about evaluating training in Chapter 8.

4. *Determine the value/cost ratio of training.* One reason training is looked upon as a nuisance rather than as a contributor to the bottom line (profit picture) of the organization is that trainers seldom develop a value/cost ratio for the training they conduct. There are few managers in an organization who, if faced with an engineering problem that is costing $100,000 a year, would balk at spending $10,000 for a solution to that problem. And yet, on all sides we receive complaints from trainers that management just will not spend any money on training.

If the training department does a thorough needs analysis and identifies the problems and the performance deficiencies, there will be many instances in which management can put a cost factor on the training needs. The major question that the trainer needs to address in value/cost analysis is: "What is the difference between the cost of no training versus the cost of training?" This means finding out what the costs (out of pocket, salary, lost business, etc.) would be if the situation continues without any solution being applied. Then an analysis and determination must be made of the cost of conducting the training that can change the situation. The difference between these two factors will usually tell both trainer and manager whether or not the training should be conducted.

TECHNIQUES OF NEEDS ANALYSIS

There are a number of techniques that can be used by trainers to determine training needs within the organization. On the following pages, we will discuss six of them:

individual interviews
group interviews
questionnaires and survey instruments
force-field analysis
critical-incident technique
behavioral scales.

Individual Interviews

One of the most common ways of gathering information in any situation is to talk to people to find out their perceptions of the problem and their ideas about the solution. Sometimes the interviews are formal; sometimes they are informal. In some cases the use of individual interviews will be the only technique used to determine the dimensions of a problem identified as having training implications. In other cases, the interviews will be just a first step. By interviewing a few people and getting an idea of what the problem is, the trainer can decide what kinds of questions need to be asked on a survey instrument in order to maximize the value of that instrument.

In order to use the interview technique most effectively, the trainer must plan the interview. This is sometimes referred to as *interviewing by objectives.* First, the interviewer must ask the question, "At the end of this series of interviews, what information will I need so that I can conduct an effective training program?" Some examples of the information that will be needed are

the exact nature of the problem
the areas affected in the organization
the number of people involved
what the performance deficiency is
what the employees are not doing that they should be doing
what the employees are doing that they should not be doing.

Once the interviewer has determined these points of information the following should be asked: "What questions do I need to ask in order to get this information?" For example, if one of the objectives is to determine the nature of the problem, some of the questions might be

Have you ever not received the information you needed?

Have you heard about other people not receiving the information they needed?

How have you received the information you need?

Once the interview is planned, that is, once the information and the questions needed are determined, the next problem is how to conduct the interview. Here are a number of helpful hints that will improve the quality of interviews.

The physical setting or the environment in which the interview is conducted is as important as the interview itself. An interview aimed at getting information or at sharing ideas should be conducted in a comfortable atmosphere. The interviewer should move away from behind a desk into a more relaxed and casual setting so that no physical barriers are placed between the interviewer and the interviewee. Ideally, the interview should be conducted on neutral grounds, such as in a conference room.

The best way to record the data from interviews differs with each individual. Most people, however, find it distracting to have the interviewer constantly writing notes. A couple of alternatives to this method are the following:

1. The interviewer can pause occasionally to give the interviewee a thought question. For example, "Think about this for a minute. If you had a chance to change the situation that you just described, what would you do?" Then while the interviewee is thinking about the question, the interviewer records whatever data are relevant from the previous few minutes. The value of this method is that the interviewee is less likely to be cued about what things are acceptable or unacceptable to the interviewer.

2. The interviewer can tape-record the entire interview. There are positive and negative aspects to this method. Some interviewees may be less candid when they know they are being recorded. One way to reduce this problem is by being as straightforward with the interviewee as possible. The interviewer should tell the interviewee that he or she wants to tape-record the information to avoid writing notes. The interviewee should be assured that no one in management, for example, will hear the tapes. By using a tape recorder with a counter on it the interviewer can avoid having to listen to the entire tape when recording the data later. The interviewer can index directly to the

spot where the salient information was given and record the information much more quickly.

A question we are often asked is how many people to interview. The answer to this is that it depends on the purpose of the interviews. If the interviews are going to be the entire source of data, more people will need to be interviewed than if the interviews are a preliminary step in the development of a questionnaire. When interviews are held with employees at the same level in the organization, we have found that a minimum of four employees should be interviewed. Ten interviews tend to be an overkill. It is not at all unusual to be able to obtain 95–98 percent of all the necessary information from the first four interviews. Experienced interviewers tell us that once they get past the fourth interview of a homogeneous group of employees, the information becomes redundant.

The way the interview is begun is of utmost importance. The first thing that needs to be done is to allay the fears and anxieties of the interviewee. The purpose of the interview should be explained fully. An example of such an explanation might be: "We have been asked by your management to develop a training program in customer relations. We said we wanted to talk to some of the people who do a good job in customer relations, and that's the reason you are here. We would like to ask you a few questions to find out what actually happens in customer relations so that the training program we develop will really be helpful."

When the interviewee is reasonably satisfied with the purpose of the interview, the first question ought to be either positive or neutral. An example of a neutral question would be: "Tell me about your job." This helps most people to talk without any problem. An example of a positive question would be: "What do you like best about your job?" Here again, the interviewee feels free to talk, and this positive question serves as a good icebreaker.

After several minutes of discussing either the neutral or the positive question the negative question can be introduced. Some examples are

"What do you feel are some of the problems in customer relations?"

"If you were allowed to make any changes that you wanted to around here, what changes would you make?"

"What are some of the problems in the organization?"

"What are some of the things that people do ineffectively in the organization?"

The interviewer should dig deeply and be intensive. Often an answer to one question does not provide the adequate information. For example, if an interviewee says that he or she was quite pleased about the previous promotion, do not assume that this is due to a desire for success (though it may well be), but rather, ask why the interviewee was pleased. The interviewer does not always have to ask a question formulated in a complete sentence. Sometimes a simple phrase, "Then what?," is enough to encourage the person to continue talking. Silence also can be a question. It implies that the listener wants to hear more.

Group Interviews

There are situations when group interviews will be more effective than individual interviews. (Generally a group of six to ten people will provide ample synergism.) Some examples are:

> If there are many employees who have information on the problem, it would be a more effective use of time to conduct 3 group interviews than to conduct 10 to 20 individual interviews.

> When the subject of the interview is one that would not cause interviewees to feel they might get into trouble if the truth were known, group interviews work well. In situations where the interviewees will be asked about their own shortcomings, individual interviews tend to be more effective than group interviews.

> When talking about other areas of the organization, that is, employees or bosses of the interviewees, or other departments, the group interview technique is very effective because the interviewees do not feel threatened by the information.

Another technique that can be used with groups to yield more information than individual interviews is *brainstorming*. It is designed to generate a great amount of data. The rules for brainstorming are these:

> 1. Limit the topic to a single question; for example, how to to deal with absenteeism.
> 2. Encourage idea quantity. At this point, quality is *not* considered important. What you are seeking is as many ideas and suggestions as possible.
> 3. Encourage wild thinking and building an idea. Any idea,

no matter how questionable, should be offered. Encourage the group to build on one another's ideas, altering them, expanding on them, and modifying them. Again, the purpose here is to get ideas, *not* pass judgment on them.

4. Discourage critical judgment and evaluation. No one is allowed to say, "That won't work because . . ." during a brainstorming session. You are looking for ways of *getting* ideas, not trying to suppress them. An idea that really will not work just might trigger someone to think of an idea that will work.

5. Avoid side discussions and issues. During the brainstorming, which is of very short duration, side discussions are not to be allowed. All members of the group are required to concentrate their energies in order to come up with additional ideas.

6. Do not allow outside observers. Everyone in the room is required to participate. It may be well to require everyone to offer at least two suggestions during the session.

7. Have an idea or two in the back of your head to get the session started. This will provide a *trigger* to get the session moving. And once it begins, the ideas come fast and furious.

8. One member of the group should take notes, recording the ideas as fast as they are offered. It is a good idea to have the suggestions listed on a chart where everyone can see them. Previous ideas provide the *food for thought* that leads to further ideas.

9. The brainstorming session itself should last not less than 5 or more than 15 minutes. Shorter periods of time do not allow enough good ideas to surface, and after 15 minutes, a greater proportion of the ideas become clearly impractical.

Just as in individual interviews, the techniques that will get the group talking must be nonthreatening. One very effective question to get a group talking about their on-the-job problems is: "What gets in the way of your doing your job as well as you would like to do it?" The answers to this question will tend to fall into three areas:

1. *The system.* The interviewees will tell about things in the system that keep them from doing their jobs as well as they would like to do it.

2. *Management.* The interviewees will talk readily about

some of the inconsistencies and poor management practices that they have observed.

3. *The interviewees themselves.* Eventually, the interviewees will get around to pointing the finger at themselves, that is, their own skill deficiencies and motivational problems, which are related to the problem being discussed.

Questionnaires and Survey Instruments

When the number of people from whom the interviewer needs to get information is too large for interviews, questionnaires and/or survey instruments can be used. They can also be used when the people to be questioned are spread over a large geographic area.

HOW TO DEVELOP AN EFFECTIVE QUESTIONNAIRE

In order to develop a questionnaire that obtains the necessary information several steps must be taken:

1. A small sample (two or three people) should be interviewed in order to learn some of the terminology and some of the general areas that the questionnaire should approach.
2. The questionnaire should be developed by using the same method as discussed in the "interviewing-by-objectives" section. The interviewer must decide what results are wanted from the questionnaire and then must identify the kinds of questions that should be asked in order to get that information.
3. The questionnaire must be tested. This is essential. It is amazing how many times we write out a question that seems very clear only to find that other people interpret it in two or three different ways.

One way to test a questionnaire or survey instrument is by getting two employees (one who is naive about the subject matter being discussed and one who is an expert on the subject) to answer the questionnaire. The trainer should sit directly across the table so that he or she can observe the expressions of the respondent; a slight hesitation, a furrowed brow, or possibly some other indication of confusion might be noted. At that point the trainer should interrupt and ask, "What's the matter?" It may be, for example, that the respondent will say, "In this question, I'm not sure what you mean by 'the work group.' Are you talking about the people in my office or are you talking about the whole plant?" This kind of feedback will allow the trainer to reword the question so that the possibility of misinterpretation is reduced.

If the number of questionnaires to be sent out is large (200 or more), we strongly recommend that the questionnaire be tested even beyond the method just described. The trainer should send the questionnaire to 10 or 20 people and when the results come in, analyze them carefully. It is often the case that people in various parts of the organization will read the questions differently, and, therefore, the information will not be helpful. The trainer may discover that some questions are leading by the pattern of responses. All positive or all negative responses should indicate some suspicion of the way the question is worded.

CHARACTERISTICS OF A QUESTIONNAIRE

• *Confidentiality.* One of the most important things that must be remembered by someone using a questionnaire is that there is a potential for anxiety about the confidentiality of the questionnaire on the part of the respondents. In some cases, we have found an unfortunate history of a lack of confidentiality on the part of the people conducting surveys. When we approached a group, we were greeted by comments like, "Hey, we're not going to tell you anything. Two years ago they conducted a survey around here and a short time afterward, three people got fired."

When a survey questionnaire is conducted, it is important that the respondents be given every assurance of confidentiality. In addition to verbal assurances, there are a number of techniques that can be used in order to give the impression of confidentiality so that the real information can be obtained from those who are completing the instrument.

One commonly used technique is to assign respondents a code number or to allow them to write a five-digit code number in the corner of the questionnaire. They keep a copy of the five-digit code number so that when they complete a second questionnaire at a later date, the trainer will not have to identify who wrote which questionnaire by name but can simply match up the code numbers in the before and after.

Another technique is to avoid asking for any biographical data on the questionnaire. If biographical data is necessary (that is, if the trainer needs to know from what levels in the organization the people are coming, from what age group, from what sex group, etc.), rather than asking a question that pinpoints age exactly, the trainer can ask the respondent to denote the age bracket into which he or she falls; for example, an alternative to

"Please state your age _____,"

would be

"Check off the age bracket into which you fall.
(a) under 25   (b) 25 to 40
(c) 40 to 55   (d) over 55."

Respondents to questionnaires that contain biographical information often feel that they have been pinpointed (and, in fact, an unscrupulous trainer could identify most of the respondents through their biographical data). Usually the need for accurate data on the important questions in the questionnaire outweighs the need for identifying the individual respondents.

Another important fact about confidentiality should be kept in mind. When a trainer goes into an organization and collects data in a needs analysis, that information is the property of the client, that is, the manager of the department. A major concern (based on our previous experiences) is that someone within the personnel department, knowing that the trainer is collecting data on department X, may see this as a convenient way to get information about department X. The trainer cannot be successful in collecting data unless he or she is trusted, and it is the trainer's responsibility to gain this trust by vigorously protecting the confidentiality of the data.

• *Closing the Loop.* Another important characteristic of an effective questionnaire is that the people who have given information somehow should be brought back into the loop. (The communications loop refers to the flow of information and feedback. When someone gives information, the first half of the loop is formed. When the giver of the information gets feedback, reaction, or evaluation, the second half of the loop is formed, and the loop is closed.) When participants do not receive any feedback about the results of the questionnaire or interviews, they may greet subsequent attempts with hostility or, at best, indifference. Therefore, we believe it is essential that the loop be closed. The minimum that should be done is that a letter be sent to all those who participated in the questionnaire or interviews thanking them for their participation and assuring them that the information they gave will be used productively, that is, in a training program or in a reengineering of the organization.

This is the *very least* that should be done. We recommend, however, something more. Once the data have been analyzed and some general trends have been seen, we strongly recommend that some or all of the information be shared with the people who participated in the survey. This can be done through a letter or through small group meetings. It is not necessary that every item be fed back to the participants. This, in fact, would be far more than they need or want to know. However, the important trends should be shared with the participants.

One concern we often encounter when we work with trainers and managers, is: "If you ask people for information and they tell you things that you can't do anything about, you are going to be worse off than if you had not asked them for information in the first place." We strongly disagree with this kind of thinking because it assumes that people are unreasonable. The problem can be avoided by feeding back the results of the survey to the people in the following three categories. The first two categories will probably constitute less than one-quarter of all the data received and the third will constitute the majority of the information.

1. *Information about which management can do something immediately.* This is exactly the way the data should be reported. "Here are some things you told us and here are the steps we have already taken in order to improve the situation you brought to our attention."

2. *Information about which management can do nothing.* "There were several things, as you might expect, that we received complaints about which, unfortunately, we are just stuck with. For example, 83 percent of the respondents complained that the parking lot on the other side of the railroad tracks is inconvenient, particularly in wet or snowy weather. We recognize the problem but we are just not able to do anything about it."

This kind of straightforward feedback is generally received positively. The participants recognize the validity of management's inability to change the situation and, yet, they feel very positive about the fact that their complaint has been registered, recognized, and, in fact, understood.

3. *Information about which management can do something but requires further information or specific planning.* "Here are some problem areas you pinpointed in the organization, and management is currently working on them. We have set up task forces to deal with each of these areas, and as results become known we will be feeding these back to you through your supervisors."

SOME TIPS FOR WRITING A QUESTIONNAIRE

We are constantly given questionnaries to review and in all of them we find the same problems. They are either too skimpy and lack adequate direction, or they are too complex in layout and cannot be understood, or they are written in a style and language so difficult one needs a Ph.D. to understand them. Here are a few hints we often pass on to questionnaire designers:

1. Write explicit instructions so that the respondents will know exactly what to do. An example follows.
   a. Read each of the statements below carefully. Circle SD if you *strongly disagree,* D if you *disagree,* A if you *agree,* and SA if you *strongly agree.*"

2. Provide a space after each question for a comment from the respondents when appropriate.

3. Be sure that the respondents can validly answer the questions. Some examples follow.
   a. "Is the personnel department responsive to the needs and problems of employees?" This question calls for a judgment about others. It would be better for each respondent to comment about himself or herself;
   "Has the personnel department been responsive to your needs and problems?"
   b. "Does your supervisor spend sufficient time writing your performance appraisal?" This question calls for an opinion that employees cannot really make. It might be better to prepare a question about the value of the appraisal.

4. Be specific. Some examples follow.
   a. "Was the training relevant to your department's needs?" More information can be obtained if a question that requires more than a Yes/No response is asked, such as, "Which training programs were relevant to your department's needs?"
   b. "Make any general or specific comments you would like about our service program." This question is too general to obtain good feedback. It might be better to ask:
   "What suggestions do you have to improve our service?"
   "What is the longest time you had to wait for service?"
   "Have you ever had to return any item we serviced? Explain."

    c. "Are the order forms beneficial to you? "In this question "beneficial" is vague. It might be better to ask how the forms are used on the job or what problems employees are having with the forms.

5. Highlight negatives to reduce the likelihood of someone misreading the question. An example follows.

    a. "What parts of the program were *not* relevant to your work situation?"

6. Ask one question at a time. Some examples follow.

    a. "Do you get the information you need to do your job or should there be more interdepartmental reports, staff meetings, and "blue letters" from the chairman?" This question could be rewritten thus:

"Do you get the information you need to do your job?"
        ( ) Yes   ( ) No

"Put a check in the appropriate column to indicate how helpful each of the following was in getting information to you."

	INADE-QUATE	HELP-FUL	VERY HELPFUL
1. Interdepartmental reports			
2. Staff meetings			
3. "Blue letters" from Chairman			

"Explain each item you checked as inadequate."

    b. "Were the training materials understandable and pertinent to your job?" This question should really be broken down into two separate questions, one about "understandable," and the other about "pertinent."

7. Use descriptive terms to help participants answer questions that have a scale. An example follows.

    a. "How much responsibility do you feel toward your new job as compared to your last job?"

1	2	3	4	5
much less	less	about the same	more	much more

Force-field Analysis

The *force-field analysis* is a technique for getting information from groups. It is derived from the principles of equilibrium found in hydraulics. For example, in Figure 2.4 the item being analyzed, absenteeism, can be represented by a single vertical line. This single vertical line represents the current state of affairs, that is, how much of the item under discussion actually exists. This line represents an equilibrium because there are causing forces acting upon it on the one hand with an equal pressure of restraining forces acting upon it on the other hand. For example, if we were to analyze absenteeism within one organization, we may find that these factors are causing forces: extensive overtime, hunting season, inaccessibility of the plant, and so on. We may find that these factors are restraining forces: perfect attendance pins, follow-up calls by personnel, threat of firing, and so on.

By getting a group together to brainstorm on a subject using the force-field analysis framework, a good deal of useful information can be obtained. The technique is simple. The only materials necessary are a pencil and flip chart paper for recording everything that is said. The interviewer starts by drawing a line down the center of the paper and then draws two arrows, one on the causing side and one on the restraining side. Then the group members are asked to call out the factors that affect the question at hand and to identify on which side they should be written. The trainer should avoid paraphrasing what each participant says: comments should be written verbatim. This avoids the problem of misinterpreting what each person has said and also seems to have a very positive effect on the responsiveness of the participants.

With a particularly active group it may be necessary for two people to record the data: one to write the information as quickly as possible and the other to listen to the group to make sure that none of the items is missed. When one sheet of paper becomes

ABSENTEEISM

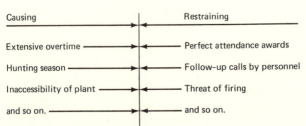

Figure 2.4 An Example of a Force-field Analysis

filled, the person who is doing the writing can post it while the other person takes over the writing chore. It is important that the written comments are visible to everyone so that they stimulate the thinking of the group.

One common complaint about the force-field analysis is that often the items listed are things over which the participants have no control. A technique for overcoming this problem is for the interviewer to identify two or three of the important items on either the causing or the restraining side and conduct another force-field analysis on those items. For example, if we were analyzing absenteeism and one of the factors identified as a causing factor was "lack of public transportation," we could conduct another force-field analysis to identify the causing and restraining factors that contribute to the lack of public transportation. In some cases a third force-field analysis is necessary before the trainer can identify a specific factor that can be changed.

To analyze data received in a force-field analysis, an uncomplicated model appears to be extraordinarily effective. It also is based on the hydraulics principle that when two equal pressures are on a line (resulting in a state of equilibrium), in order to move the line in one direction, either more pressure must be added to one side or some pressure released from the other side. More movement for energy expended can be obtained if the release method is used than if the adding method is used. It is our belief that this same principle works in human relations. We can obtain more results if we remove the obstacles holding back the positive performance than if we add more causative factors to the positive performance. Conversely, we can affect more behavior change if we remove the obstacles that are causing negative performance than if we add more pressures to the positive performance. Figure 2.5 illustrates this point.

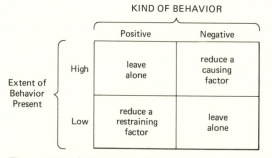

Figure 2.5   A Model for Using the Force-field Analysis

Let us look at some specific examples. Suppose we are talking about absenteeism, which in the chart above is a negative behavior. If we look at the organization and find little absenteeism, our recommendation would be to do nothing about it. If, on the other hand, we examine the organization and find a great deal of absenteeism, the best approach would be to remove or to reduce one of the causing factors rather than to increase some of the restraining factors. For example, we would have more effect on absenteeism if we started a bus line than if we added more pressure for surveillance on the part of the supervisors.

On the other hand, we would do just the opposite if the factor under investigation were positive, for example, sales volume. If our examination shows that sales are high in the organization, our recommendation would be to do nothing about it. If, on the other hand, we find that sales are too low, then our recommendation would be to reduce or to remove one of the restraining factors: eliminate or reduce something that is holding down sales.

It should be noted that in both of the preceding examples our approach to improve the situation is to remove rather than to add.

PRESENTING FORCE-FIELD CONCEPTS

Trainers can lose credibility by using jargon. The force-field analysis techniques we have just described can be used without ever using the phrases "force-field analysis," "causing factors," or "restraining factors."

A technique for obtaining the necessary information without using the training jargon can be broken down into three steps.

1. The trainer should first ask the group to identify the goal: "What is it that we are trying to accomplish?" (*Note:* When we identify a goal we are looking at a positive factor in terms of the model given in Figure 2-5.)

2. Next the trainer should draw an arrow toward the goal and ask the group to answer this question: "What are we doing that is moving us toward the goal? What are the things we are doing correctly?" For the next several minutes the group should brainstorm answers to that question. Once this is done the answers should be posted.

3. The trainer then should draw the arrow in the opposite direction and ask, "What are the things that we are doing that are keeping us from achieving our goal?" The group's responses to this question should be written down. It has

been our experience that the things that we are doing that keep us from achieving a goal will outnumber the things that we are doing correctly by three or four to one. There are more ways of doing something wrong than there are of doing it correctly.

Because the goal has been stated in positive terms, when the group finally begins to do something to improve the situation, "restraining forces" should be the focus of their attention. By following this model a trainer can get the restraining and causing factors in a force-field analysis without ever using the jargon.

HOW TO ANALYZE DATA

One of the problems with using a force-field analysis is that the data are not quantifiable. Qualitative data require a different approach to analysis. When presenting data from a force-field analysis to management, the trainer should list all of the positive and negative comments and try to identify those comments that carry the most weight. Since a very important item or a very unimportant item would both be mentioned only one time in the force-field analysis technique, it is necessary to enlist the aid of management in identifying the relative importance of these items. Further analysis is then done through individual interviews or questionnaires to get an accurate assessment of a problem area.

Also, the data should be presented in categories that can be understood readily and that become the focus of change. For example, when dealing with supervisor-subordinate relations, the trainer might use categories such as

information sharing
involvement in decisions
feedback
communications
interest or listening.

Critical-Incident Technique

The *critical-incident technique* is one of the more interesting ways of doing a needs analysis. It is based on the 80/20 principle; that is, a large percentage of a person's effectiveness depends on a small percentage of his or her behaviors. The critical-incident technique is designed to identify those important behaviors.

A critical-incident questionnaire can be either positive or negative and usually contains only three questions. For example, a positive critical-incident form would include the following questions:

1. Name something that a person in this position has done that you would classify as outstanding behavior.
2. What led up to this incident?
3. What were the results?

A negative critical-incident form would be similar and would include the following questions:

1. Name something that a person in this position did that you would consider very ineffective.
2. What led up to this incident?
3. What were the results?

Critical-incident forms are sent to members of the target population, supervisors of the target population, and peers or subordinates with whom the target population interface. Generally, each person will submit a maximum of six incidents (three positive and three negative). When the answers are received, the trainer will have a collection of the most important behaviors and also those that a person should avoid in order to be effective on that job. The trainer could then design a program based on teaching people to do things on the positive side and to avoid doing things on the negative side.

Just as important as the list of the positive and negative behaviors are the details in the incidents themselves. A trainer with some imagination and creativity will be able to design case studies, role plays, and trigger films using the information gleaned from the critical incidents. An excellent learning design can be built around reading the critical incident to the group and leading a discussion of the pros and cons of the incident.

As in the case of sorting qualitative comments from a force-field analysis, the data from a critical-incident questionnaire should also be grouped into major categories. The trainer should read each incident and sort it into a pile with other similar incidents; categories should not be made before the sorting begins or items may be forced into categories. After all incidents are sorted a second reading should be held if necessary to be sure all groups are common. Typical categories for a production supervisor's job will be safety, employee relations, equipment, union relations, administrative work, among numerous others.

Behavioral Scales

Another technique akin to the critical-incident technique is the use of *behavioral scales*. This may be a misnomer. The technique became valuable as a needs analysis strategy in a project aimed at developing a performance appraisal system that was to be based on behaviors scaled from high to low.

The objective of the behavioral scales is to identify a long list of specific behaviors done by the target population. For example, to design a training program for first-line supervisors in a manufacturing plant, the trainer would develop a list of things that the supervisors do by categories: production, safety, labor relations, and so on. A step-by-step procedure to obtain this list follows:

1. The trainer meets with a group of about 10 first-line supervisors and asks them each to write a statement of an outstanding behavior (observable and measurable) that they have done or that they have seen another first-line supervisor do.

2. The trainer gives the group a few minutes to try writing such a statement.

3. The statements are read to the group and the trainer points out which of the statements are observable and measurable, which of them pertain to the target population, and which of them are single incidents.

4. Once the positive statements have been critiqued, the group is told to write a statement of a supervisor's behavior that they thought was very poor.

5. These statements are also analyzed and critiqued. At this point it is expected that the participants will understand the technique.

6. Then the trainer asks the group to answer what is probably the most difficult question: "State a single observable behavior of a first-line supervisor that you consider to be average performance." (This usually is difficult because it is easier to think of examples of outstanding or poor behavior than of "average" behavior.)

7. Once again, these statements are critiqued to make sure that they are, in fact, examples of a first-line supervisor's observable behavior.

8. At this point, the trainer tells the participants to start writing as many statements as they can about positive, negative, or average performances. Depending on the

time available, the group will be able to develop a long list of behaviors.

The same procedure should be repeated with a group of supervisors of the target population. If the trainees are first-line supervisors, general supervisors or superintendents should be brought in. A third group that can be helpful in developing behavioral statements about a group of potential trainees are those with whom the target population interface. In the first-line production supervisor example, the trainer can bring in people from quality control, material handling, personnel, accounting, and so on, and ask them the same kinds of questions.

At the end of this experience, the trainer will have a long list of specific behaviors of the target population. The next step is to group them into the categories of work in which the target population is engaged, for example, production, safety, quality control, interpersonal relations, labor relations, housekeeping, and so on. Then all the participants who made the original statements should evaluate each behavior on a scale of 1 to 9 (1 indicating horrible performance, perhaps worthy of dismissal or certainly discipline, and 9 indicating outstanding performance, worthy of commendation). If there are a large number of statements, from as many as 30 people, a computer may be necessary to tabulate the data. The trainer will end up with a list of behaviors of the target population organized into categories and ranked from the very best behaviors down through the very worst behaviors.

For trainers, then, the objective is to train toward the things at the top of the list and to train away from the things at the bottom of the list. These, in fact, can provide ready-made objectives for a training program.

Perhaps the most interesting part will be the items that rank in the middle. Many of these items will not be true average behaviors but will have an average score because some participants rated them high and others rated them low. These behavioral statements are the controversial ones, which lend themselves to active discussions. Excellent training materials can be developed around behavioral statements on which there was no agreement or on which the target population agreed but their supervisors had different ideas. These items guarantee lively discussion and the exposure of diverse views.

An example of a controversial statement is one written about a first-line supervisor in an automobile assembly plant: "He went into the drying oven, picked up two fenders, and ran them back 50 yards to the line in time to be put on the car." The ratings on this statement ranged from 1 to 9. There was no agreement whatever as to whether it was a positive or a negative behavior. Those emphasizing the production aspects of the job saw it as a very positive behavior; those looking at the safety aspects of the job (if he had slipped in the bake oven, he might have been killed) saw it as a negative behavior. Some saw it as a violation of the union-management contract, while others seemed to think it was a standard behavior and not worthy of note. We conducted a two-hour training program on the responsibilities of a supervisor simply by having the participants discuss this specific statement.

DATA CONFRONTATION

The typical trainer is at an organizational level that does not give him or her the clout to confront managers personally. Most trainers we have talked to see it as suicidal to approach a high-ranking manager and say, "I think you've got problems in your organization, and here's what you ought to do about it." A more effective and far safer technique is the use of *data confrontation*.

The essence of data confrontation is that the trainer does not have to confront the manager personally, but rather shares the data received and lets the manager confront the data. There is no need for the trainer to say, "Your people are unhappy" if the results of the questionnaire point out that 87 percent of the people would transfer if it were not for the poor economic situation. The data speak for themselves and are powerful; they are objective, measurable, and, in many cases, irrefutable.

Presenting the Data to Management

In addition to avoiding personal confrontation by using data to confront management, there are several other things that a trainer should do in order to be more effective in this phase of the job.

1. When getting the approval of the manager to conduct the needs analysis, the trainer must make it clear that after the data have been put together, the trainer and manager both share the data.

2. The trainer should meet first with the top manager of the department to share the data and then let the manager share the information with subordinate managers, with the trainer working

as a process attendant. This is especially important when some of the data are sensitive. It would be politically foolhardy to have the top manager in the organization be surprised by the data. By meeting with the trainer in advance and by getting some recommendations for solutions, the manager can go into a meeting with subordinate managers from a position of strength. The support received from the subordinate managers will be enhanced tremendously through this technique.

3. Training jargon should be avoided. Actions taken should be stated simply and directly. For example, instead of saying, "We conducted a needs analysis," the trainer can say, "We talked with some of your people in groups of eight or nine and here's what they told us."

4. The trainer should have recommendations ready. Most managers, after reviewing the data, will ask the question, "What can we do about it?" Have alternative responses available to share with management.

CONCLUSION

The effectiveness of the training function lies in the trainer's ability to solve problems that result in payback to the organization. This will be done consistently only if a great deal of the effort expended on any given "program" goes into needs analysis. It is not at all uncommon for the real solution to a problem to be found in systems and organizational files, not in training. Often changing the behavior of a target group of nonperformers or underperformers does not involve training the target group but involves training their superiors.

Various forms of needs analysis are available to the trainer, and in all cases the target population and the supervisors of the target population must be involved. Also, all formats of needs analysis provide data needed to demonstrate to management the significance or extent of a problem and also provide the "before" data for later evaluation efforts.

Additional Reading

1. *Analyzing Performance Problems,* Mager, R. F., and Pipe, P., Belmont, Calif.: Fearon, 1970.
2. "Praxeonomy: A Systematic Approach to Identifying Training Needs," Gilbert, T. F., *Management of Personnel Quarterly,* Vol. 6, No. 3, Fall, 1967.

3. *Behavior Analysis and Management,* Harless, J. H., Champagne, Ill.: Stipes, 1970.
4. *Survey Guided Development II: A Manual for Consultants,* Hausser, D. L., Pecorella, P. A., Wissler, A. L., La Jolla, Calif.: University Associates, Inc., 1977.

Chapter 3
Task Analysis

WHAT IS A TASK ANALYSIS

Simply speaking, a *task analysis* is a method the trainer uses to determine the specific components of a job in order to identify what an employee really does. Stated another way, task analysis is a method for specifying in precise detail and in measurable terms the human performance required to achieve specific management objectives, the tools and conditions needed to perform the job, and the skills and knowledge required of the employee.

WHY CONDUCT A TASK ANALYSIS

There are many reasons for conducting a task analysis. They are as follows:

1. For trainers, the primary reason for conducting a task analysis is to develop an effective training program. The task analysis divides the job into parts so that the performance of each part can be described and measured. Then the learning and skills required for each part of the job can be identified. The task analysis helps trainers focus on these important questions: (a) What should be

taught in the course? (b) What kind of test should be used to measure achievement? (c) How can the trainer ensure that what is taught in the training program will be transferred to the job? (d) How can the results be measured?

2. The task analysis provides trainees with a step-by-step description of what they are expected to do on the job. In addition, the trainees are given additional information, such as what tools will be needed, what the conditions are under which they will have to work, and the relative importance of the tasks.

3. Task analysis provides management with objective and measurable criteria of job performance. This assists management in identifying problems of job performance and in conducting performance appraisals.

Task analysis also gives management an opportunity to resolve misunderstandings that have existed in defining a particular job. Each year a number of MBA candidates earn their degrees by conducting a study in which they examine the boss's perspective of a job and the employee's perspective of the same job. It is not at all unusual to find that whereas there is some agreement, often there is a great deal of disagreement.

The task analysis allows management to identify the relative importance of each task and enables the manager and the employees to understand what really is expected.

4. Task analysis helps the personnel and training departments demonstrate more systematically to management the contribution made by the human resources department to the objectives of the organization.

5. The task analysis often is used by the industrial engineering department to work with the production and systems department to modify jobs, to simplify tasks, and to improve employee performance through job engineering.

HOW TO CONDUCT A TASK ANALYSIS

The task analysis described in this chapter probably contains more functions than most trainers will find occasion to use. It does, however, provide trainers with whatever they might need, no matter what the circumstances.

Elements of a Task Analysis

A complete task analysis system will contain the following elements:

1. a statement of the task to be performed (a task list)
2. when and how often the task is to be performed

3. the quantity and quality of the performance required
4. the conditions under which the task is to be performed
5. the importance of each task to the overall goals of the job
6. aptitudes, skills, or knowledge necessary to perform the task
7. the type of learning needed
8. the learning difficulty
9. the equipment, tools, and material needed
10. where the best place is to learn the task.

On the following pages each of these areas is discussed in detail.

An example of a task analysis recording form is shown in Figure 3.1. There are many different forms that have been developed for recording the data collected in a task analysis. The form used will depend on the purpose for doing the task analysis. The form included here is a good starting point, and, depending on the specific needs of the job for which the task analysis is being conducted, some of the sections may be eliminated if necessary.

COLUMN 1: THE TASK LIST

In the first column the major tasks and subtasks should be listed. A commonly used system assigns cardinal numbers to each of the major tasks performed on the job and decimal numbers to each of the subtasks under each major task. For example:

1   a major task
1.1 subtask
1.2 subtask
1.3 subtask
2   a new major task
2.1 subtask.

The distinction between the major task and the subtask lies in the answers to these questions:

The major task answers the question, "What is to be performed?"
The subtask answers the questions: "What are the steps that a person takes in order to perform this major task?" and "How is the major task to be performed?"

For example, a very simplified model might look like this:

1   Start an automobile.
1.1 Place the key in the ignition.

Figure 3.1   Task Analysis Record Form

TASK LIST	WHEN AND HOW OFTEN PERFORMED	QUANTITY AND QUALITY OF PER- FORMANCE	CONDITIONS UNDER WHICH PERFORMED	IMPOR- TANCE	SKILLS OR KNOWLEDGE REQUIRED	TYPES OF LEARNING TASKS INVOLVED	LEARNING DIFFICULTY	EQUIPMENT, TOOLS, AND MATERIALS NEEDED	WHERE BEST LEARNED
1									
1.1									
1.2									
1.3									
2									
2.1									

1.2 Put the selector lever in park.
1.3 Push the gas pedal to the floor.
1.4 Turn the key all the way to the right.
1.5 Allow the key to return to the center position.
1.6 Lift the foot from the gas pedal.

A *major task statement* is a principal behavior that is expected to be performed for a given job. It identifies observable behavior. The tasks should be mutually exclusive; that is, the performance of one major task is not required while others are being performed. Typically, a major task statement identifies behavior that is frequently performed. Finally, a major task is an important part of the total job.

Here are three examples of jobs and some of their major task statements:

A. Production supervisor
   1. Prepare the shift for start-up.
   2. Maintain quality.
   3. Assign employees to production operations.
   4. Order production materials.
   5. Complete a daily report of the time sheet.
   6. Read and respond to information written in the supervisor's log book.
   7. Maintain housekeeping.
   8. Train employees.
   9. Respond to grievances filed by employees.
B. Training coordinator
   1. Conduct a task analysis.
   2. Conduct a needs analysis.
   3. Design training programs.
   4. Conduct training programs.
   5. Conduct evaluations.
   6. Develop maintenance-of-behavior programs.
   7. Coordinate the apprentice program.
   8. Administer ongoing educational programs.
C. Nurse's aide
   1. Keep the rooms orderly.
   2. Maintain the nursing station supplies.
   3. Maintain the emergency equipment.
   4. Maintain the patient and ward equipment and supplies.
   5. Assist the nurse with movement, bathing, or hygienic care of patients.

Examples of the subtasks related to the major tasks are:

A. Production supervisor
  4   Order production materials.
  4.1 Using Form 171J, take a weekly inventory.
  4.2 Estimate from projected production supplies the materials needed.
  4.3 Compare needs with the inventory and prepare a storage order form, Form 171K.

B. Training coordinator
  5   Conduct evaluations.
  5.1 Identify the standards of terminal behavior.
  5.2 Working with management, identify the value of changes in behavior.
  5.3 Measure current behavior.
  5.4 Develop instruments as techniques for measuring changes in behavior.

C. Nurse's aide
  3   Maintain the emergency equipment.
  3.1 Compare the available equipment with a checklist of required equipment daily.
  3.2 Check all dates on medications, fire equipment, and so on, to assure that it is current.
  3.3 Check all the rooms for equipment preparedness as outlined in the checklist procedures.

COLUMN 2: WHEN AND HOW OFTEN PERFORMED

In this column the frequency of the task is reported. This is especially important to the trainer because those tasks that are performed frequently often require a different kind of training and reinforcement schedule from those tasks that are performed infrequently. The measures used in this column should describe as specifically as possible when and how often a task is performed: for example, is the task done at the beginning of the shift; is it done before the shift begins; is it done only in response to other specific events; is it done once a day or once every minute; is it done every Friday, every 500 miles, or every 10,000 pieces produced?

COLUMN 3: THE QUANTITY AND QUALITY OF PERFORMANCE

The information in this column is extremely important to the trainer, because it leads directly to the objectives that will be developed for a training program. It is a direct expression of the corporate, organizational, or departmental goals. Performance standards should be as specific as possible. They may refer to a time standard, for example, within two minutes or within a half-hour. This could be stated as a time range (in one to three minutes, in not more than five minutes, etc.).

The performance standard often is stated in terms of accuracy: for example, with a plus or a minus tolerance of 0.007; within 3 feet of the designated area; completely; 100 percent correct; 70 percent correct; with three out of four in the bull's eye.

COLUMN 4: CONDITIONS UNDER WHICH PERFORMED

This column will not be used always. Often the conditions under which the task is performed are not critical to the training and will not influence performance. There are some tasks and jobs, however, in which the conditions will influence the performance and the training. One example of this is decision making. In developing a program to train managers in decision making, it is important that the trainer knows the conditions under which the managers make decisions. Do the managers have considerable lead time and the option of conducting meetings with subordinates to obtain information? Or do they, given incomplete information, need to make immediate decisions? The kind of training conducted for each of these kinds of decision making would differ because of the circumstances under which the decisions are made.

For important tasks that are performed infrequently, such as safety and emergency procedures, it is necessary for the trainer to know if the conditions under which the task is performed in a real-life situation are distracting so that this can be built into the training.

Even though this column will not always be used the trainer should always investigate to make sure that special conditions do not exist.

COLUMN 5: IMPORTANCE

This column contains information important to the task analysis. By knowing the perceived importance of each task to attaining the overall objectives of the job, the trainer and managers will find it easier to make decisions about the training: for example, what kind of test should be given; should a training program be developed; is a maintenance or reinforcement program required? If the task is of major importance and perceived as such by performers and management alike, then there is no question that it must be emphasized both in the training and in the reinforcement programs. If, however, the task receives a relatively low rating in importance, job aids may be substituted readily for the training.

A simple, but effective method for identifying the importance of each task is for the trainer to set up a five-point scale in which 5 means the task is extremely important and 1 means the task is relatively less important. A survey of the employees and their supervisors that asks them to apply the five-point scale to each task will separate the very important from the less important.

COLUMN 6: SKILLS OR KNOWLEDGE REQUIRED

In this column the trainer records the things that the employee needs to know or do in order to perform the task under consideration. This is especially important, not only for the development of training exercises, but also for identifying a selection criterion. When it is used as the basis for developing training exercises, this column provides the information on the kinds of skill or knowledge required to perform the task and defines the entering behavior required to approach the specific task. For example, if a task requires that certain measurements be made on a piece of steel, the entering behavior of the trainee may include how to use the measuring instrument and being able to add.

In some cases it is difficult to make judgments about the kinds of aptitudes that are required. In most cases, however, the trainer should be able to specify the types of skills and knowledge required by observing the task being performed and carefully questioning the person performing the task.

COLUMN 7: TYPES OF LEARNING TASKS INVOLVED

This column is easier to use if the trainer has had some training in learning theory. The information recorded in this column, however, may prove to be critical in terms of designing the training exercises. The kind of task that is being performed, for example, one of recall or one of discrimination, will determine the kind of training and the kind of test that will be developed in the training program.

Beach and Mager have identified five different kinds of performance:[1]

1. *Discrimination.* Discrimination means being able to tell the difference between two or more things or to identify one thing as different from another, for example, to be able to tell when the job has been completed or when the task needs to be done, or to be able

---

[1] Kenneth M. Beach, Jr., and Robert F. Mager, *Measuring Instructional Intent* (Belmont, Calif.: Fearon Publishers, Inc., 1967).

to see the difference between what is correct and what is incorrect. Some examples of discrimination on the job are an industrial inspector determining that a product does not conform to specified standards, a landscaper identifying which branches are diseased, or a police officer recognizing that a driver has exceeded the speed limit. In these cases the performer is discriminating between what is, from either a mental or a physical image, and what ought to be.

2. *Problem Solving.* Once the performer is able to discriminate that something is incorrect or does not fit the criteria, the next step is to problem solve, that is, to identify the cause and the solution of the problem. Some on-the-job examples are a TV repair worker looks at the kind of picture being displayed in order to diagnose possible causes and then runs several simple tests to identify the specific tube or part that is causing the problem, and a supervisor talks to a poor performer trying to discover what the performer's problem is.

3. *Recall.* Whenever there are some things that the trainee "must know," then the performance is based on recall, for example: an employee must know the names of parts or tools; or a manager must remember a list of "do's and don't's" in interviewing. Sometimes the recall is simple, such as seeing an item and recalling its name. Sometimes the recall is not so simple, as in sequencing or *chaining.* An example of chaining is remembering the alphabet: when we recite the alphabet, we recall that "A" is the first letter, and then "A" triggers the second recall that "B" follows "A," and "B" triggers the third recall that "C" follows "B," and so forth. The same thing happens when we remember a procedure, for example, how to perform mouth-to-mouth resuscitation, how to conduct a disciplinary hearing, or how to take a set of fingerprints from a suspect.

Although the process of recall is an internal, mental one, it can be identified in relation to a visible activity, for example, reciting or writing the names of items. Whenever the principal feature of a task is that it requires knowing what to do more than how to do it, the performance becomes one primarily of recall.

4. *Manipulation.* Knowing what to do is not the same thing as knowing how to do a task. For example, a supervisor may know that an upset employee needs to be calmed down, but knowing *how* to calm down the employee is a different matter. This may seem obvious, but it needs to be emphasized because sometimes trainers fail to follow theory with practice; they believe that if trainees know what to do, they will be able to do it. In motivation training, for

example, some trainers teach the five levels of needs on the Maslow Needs Hierarchy.[2] When the trainee is able to recall those five different levels, the trainer walks away assuming that the trainee will be able to use the Needs Hierarchy in order to motivate employees.

5. *Speech.* For many operations speech is merely a form of communicating a piece of information. Some tasks, however, require that speech be used in a special way; for example, in the case of a sales representative, a telephone operator, or an order clerk, the way in which the person speaks is essential to success, so appropriate instruction must be included in the training program. In one sense speech is similar to manipulation except that manipulation tends to be a physical activity whereas speech is an oral activity.

There are different instructional methods and media appropriate to each kind of performance task. In Chapter 5 we will discuss each of these types of performance in terms of program design.

COLUMN 8: LEARNING DIFFICULTY

In this column the trainer should record how difficult it is for an average person to learn to perform the task at a level of competency. The most common way of doing this is again by using a scale, for example, 1 to 5 (1 means the task is very simple and 5 means it is extremely difficult). This information usually can be obtained from employees who recently have learned the task or who currently are engaged in learning the task.

This information is helpful to the trainer in making a decision (along with the data on task frequency and importance of task) concerning how much time and expense should be expended in order to train the employees in various tasks.

COLUMN 9: EQUIPMENT, TOOLS, AND MATERIALS NEEDED

Although this column is not critical to the task analysis, it helps the trainer to systematize the collection of data in order to make sure that nothing is overlooked. It may be essential if the trainer is setting up a learning laboratory. Usually learning how to use a complicated tool or piece of equipment will be covered as a separate subtask.

COLUMN 10: WHERE BEST LEARNED

In this column the trainer makes a decision as to whether the task can be learned best in a classroom session or on the job. In some

[2] A. H. Maslow, "A Theory of Human Motivation," *Psychological Review,* 50 (1943): 370–396.

cases it may be decided that ability to perform a task should be a selection criteria for a specific job.

In determining whether the task can be best taught in the classroom or on the job, the trainer should consider several factors:

Are there cognitive parts to the task; that is, does the trainee need to *know* something before he or she can perform the task? (If the answer is yes, then some classroom training probably is required.)

Is the task so simple that it can be observed once and then be done correctly? (If the answer is yes, then the training probably should be done on the job.)

Is the task complicated? (If the answer is yes, then it probably should be broken down into easily learned segments and learned in the classroom, perhaps utilizing laboratory methods or simulators.)

Can the equipment, materials, and situations be duplicated for classroom training? (If the answer is no, or if duplication is too expensive, a combination of classroom and on the job training is most practical.)

Can realism and job conditions be duplicated or simulated in the classroom? (If the answer is yes, especially for positions demanding high interpersonal ability, classroom training using experience-based methods may be best, since this allows learning and practice in a low-risk setting. If not, then on-the-job observation, training, and teaching will be needed.)

METHODS OF IDENTIFYING TASKS

Several techniques are available to the trainer for identifying tasks. Among them are literature search, interviews, questionnaires and surveys, direct observation, hardware analysis, and critical-incident techniques (discussed in Chapter 2). Most trainers who conduct task analyses use a combination of methods, because any one of the methods used alone has weaknesses that may be detrimental to the results of the final analysis. By using several methods, the weakness of the primary method can be offset.

We will take a look at each one of these methods and discuss the details of how, with whom, and when to use each.

Literature Search

Depending on the job being analyzed, a good deal of information may be available in the literature. Many companies have conducted task analyses on jobs such as first-line production supervisor, secretary, designer, and so on. In most cases a good deal can be learned about the job by reading these task analyses. Because of the nuances within various kinds of organizations, however (e.g., governmental versus production versus service), the amount of information learned from reading these task analyses may not be sufficient.

Some of the more valuable sources of information on tasks include textbooks from university or technical programs, packaged training materials, civil service examination books, government (especially Department of Labor) studies, and even narratives from career planning publications.

Another source is the job descriptions that many organizations issue for every job. One word of caution is necessary here: recognize that the purpose for most job descriptions is not for training but for justifying financial or salary planning decisions. The descriptions identify the duties, responsibilities, reporting relationships, authority, and so on, of the jobs to justify a certain salary grade and pay level. It is not at all unusual to find that most of the things a person does on the job are included in a final statement of the job description, "Complete any other tasks as necessary."

Doing a literature search will acquaint the trainer with some of the features of the job so that during an interview he or she will know what to observe or at least will have some idea of what kinds of questions to ask. The task analysis generally will be improved if the trainer is not totally naive about the operation.

Interviews

Interviews are probably the most commonly used method for accumulating data in a task analysis. The trainer interviews supervisors or employees or both. The supervisor should be interviewed before the employees for two reasons: first, because the supervisor ought to know what is happening with subordinates, and second, because the supervisor can offer information on how the job *should be done*. (It is important to recognize that this may not be the way the job is now being done.) The interview with the supervisor will also help to remove some of the trainer's naivete, so that when talks are held with employees, the interchange will be more fruitful.

The question of how many people should be interviewed on the job cannot be answered with a general statement. It depends, of course, on how many employees there are on the job and how many are available. If there are just a few people on the job, they all should be interviewed. Most likely, however, a task analysis would not be conducted for the job unless there were a relatively large number of employees.

We have often found that interviewing only four to six employees will give most of the necessary information to the interviewer. Interviewing additional people tends to be repetitive and, we might add, very boring. There might be some reasons, however, for interviewing more than just four people, for example, there may be a need to involve larger numbers of people in order to make sure that every one feels included in the project.

When an interview is used in developing a task analysis, we prefer that the trainer use the steps below in the following order:

1. Interview the supervisors of the people doing the job.
2. Interview the employees.
3. Summarize the tasks reported by the supervisor and the employees.
4. Meet with the supervisors (and perhaps some of the employees) to review the task lists. This helps to ensure that major points have not been overlooked or that undue emphasis has not been put on one facet of the job. It also allows the interviewees a second chance at remembering what it is they do on the job. We often find that in this validation meeting some new and important information is added. This seems to happen particularly with some of the cyclical tasks that occur only annually or semiannually.

ADVANTAGES OF INTERVIEWS

There are a number of advantages in using direct interviews:

The interviewer can ask questions to clarify the meaning of terms and tasks.

The interviewer can evaluate the quality of the task list.

The interviewer can concentrate only on task identification and avoid extraneous detail.

The interviewer can establish a rapport with the supervisor and the workers and thus pick up "inside bits of information" that may not be available through a questionnaire.

There are, however, some disadvantages to the direct interview method:

Interviewing is a time consuming process. This is particularly true if a large number of people have to be interviewed.

Interviewing requires that workers be taken off their jobs. From management's point of view, this often is the major disadvantage to interviews.

Interviewing is necessarily limited to relatively small numbers of people. For example, it would be most unlikely that more than 20 people would be interviewed in any task analysis. The questionnaire, on the other hand, could be administered to an almost limitless number of people.

WHOM TO INTERVIEW

We strongly believe in interviewing the "master in the system," that is, the one, two, or three performers who in the opinion of management are doing the job the way it should be done. One word of caution is worth mentioning here. It is possible that some of the mavericks in the system, that is, those people who are seen by management as troublemakers, may, in fact, have some very important contributions to make about how the job ought to be done or about shortcuts on the job. Also, some who are considered masters may not really be masters on the job, but instead, masters at pleasing the boss. This is difficult to check, but should be watched for.

Many trainers recommend that when conducting a task analysis, some of the excellent performers as well as some of the poor performers be interviewed. We see little value in this. A poor performer says things that are not very different from what an excellent performer says. The fact of the matter is that poor performers think they are doing things that they really do not do. Or, often, it is not in what is done, but in how the job is done that the difference between the excellent and the poor performer is identified. Thus, talking with the poor performers is generally a waste of time.

Questionnaires and Surveys

We have already discussed in considerable detail in the previous chapter how to develop, prepare, distribute, and summarize a questionnaire. In terms of a task analysis, we suggest that the questionnaire either be designed with the aid of someone who is knowledgeable about the job or after a few people have been interviewed. Once the results of the questionnaire have been summarized, the trainer should review them for accuracy and completeness with the supervisors and some of the masters in the system. Otherwise, there is a danger that the trainer who probably is not knowledgeable about the job will misinterpret much of the data.

There are two advantages to the questionnaire and survey method:

It saves time. This, of course, assumes that the development of the questionnaire is not an elaborate process.

It can be used for a large number of people.

There are, however, a few disadvantages to the questionnaire and survey method:

It does not permit direct investigation of meaning: when something is written that the trainer does not understand, the trainer has no opportunity to question the person who wrote it.

The trainer may be confused as to what is expected on the job compared to what really is done on the job.

There is a tendency for people, when writing about their jobs, to say what ought to be done rather than what they actually do.

Direct Observation

Direct observation of tasks being performed is the most valid and, in some cases, the most desirable method of conducting a task analysis. There are, however, some problems that can arise and that need to be avoided. One of these is that some employees may be concerned when they see a stranger watching them work. It is essential that the person being observed should not be concerned about why somebody is watching. A meeting with all the people who are going to be involved (and this probably includes union representatives) can help in overcoming this hurdle. We also recommend that the supervisor introduce the trainer to the person who is doing the job and indicate that it is not a test, that the job will not be changed, and that, in fact, the person being observed has been chosen because he or she is one of the better performers.

We recommend that trainers who conduct task analyses use direct observation as a validation method. After they have determined through interviews or a questionnaire or both what the tasks of the job are, they observe several workers on the job to make sure that what they were told is what the workers actually do.

There are two advantages to the direct observation method:

The trainer sees exactly what the worker does on the job.

The trainer sees the way in which tools and instruments are used on the job.

However, there are a few disadvantages to the direct observation method:

Observation is expensive and not always practical or possible. Many jobs have cyclical operations that occur once a week, once a month, or once a year. It would be difficult to observe these operations for a long enough period of time to see all of them.

The trainer may not see emergency situations, which arise without any predetermined schedule, while observing the operations.

One of the most creative task analyses that we have seen was conducted by a different version of the direct observation method; it concerned a production supervisor's job in an automobile engine plant. In this situation the trainer who was going to develop the training program actually had worked as a supervisor for approximately three months. He kept a detailed diary of his activities while he was learning the job. At the end of that time, he had a good idea of what the job entailed, but more importantly, he had excellent insight into the things a new supervisor wants and needs to know. Consequently, the training program that he developed turned out to be very useful to the new supervisors.

Hardware Analysis

When a new piece of equipment is ordered, the task analysis can be conducted by analyzing the hardware. As a matter of fact, with most equipment, especially if it is expensive, the vendor may have already developed a task list that can be used for training the operators on the job. A phone call or a visit to the organization from which the equipment was purchased can save the trainer a good deal of time and effort. The trainer should always take a tape recorder and a small camera on these visits and ask many questions and take many pictures (assuming prior approval to do so is obtained).

ALTERNATIVE APPROACHES TO WRITING THE TASK ANALYSIS

The method the trainer decides to use will depend upon the job being analyzed. Some jobs lend themselves to one method more readily than others. There are three principal approaches to writing a task analysis:

1. chronological order
2. job responsibilities
3. task frequency.

Chronological Order

One way to conduct the task analysis is to record each task an employee does in *chronological order,* that is, in the order in which he or she does it. This method can be used to analyze positions where the tasks are routine, repetitive, or cyclical. The kind of job that lends itself to the chronological-order method tends to be one in which there is a good deal of physical activity, as opposed to intellectual activity, for example, assembly line operations, welding operations, or keypunch operations.

There are several advantages to approaching a task analysis using the chronological-order method:

It maintains the order in which the tasks will be performed on the job.

It is easier for the employee to review the task list to check for omissions.

The employees can be observed while they are performing the tasks to make sure they do what they have said they do.

The major disadvantage of this method is that the same task will be recorded as it is performed at different times throughout the day, and this can become very repetitive.

Job Responsibilities

Another way to approach a task analysis is to list the job responsibilities. This works particularly well when the job includes a combination of mutually exclusive tasks and when there is no predetermined order for performing the tasks. Some examples of jobs of this sort are the secretary's job of typing, filing, taking phone messages, taking dictation, and so on, or the automobile mechanic's job of changing the oil and filter, changing the brake lining, lubricating the automobile, and so on. It is apparent that many of these tasks are simply subtasks of the job and that at some point each subtask will have to be broken down further on the task list for actual training design.

The advantages to setting up a task analysis according to job responsibilities are:

The same tasks are not repeated on the list.

The performance of the job may provide natural groupings that will lend themselves to the training design.

The major disadvantage of this kind of approach is that it is easy to overlook a group of tasks, particularly ones that are not performed on a daily or a weekly basis.

Task Frequency

A third way to approach a task analysis is by noting the frequency in which the tasks are conducted. This is particularly useful when the job is not dependent upon a predetermined order for performing tasks and exclusively reactive to the work environment.

Examples of this kind of job would be a retail sales representative, a receptionist, or an electrical maintenance worker.

The advantages of using the task frequency approach are:

The tasks that occur most frequently are listed first, which gives them primary importance.

The rank order of the task frequency list can be used in developing a learning design; that is, the tasks that are most important can receive emphasis in the training.

The major disadvantage of using the task frequency technique is that there probably are some tasks that are seldom performed but are extremely important. An example of this might be an employee's handling of an emergency situation. A flight attendant, for example, serves a great deal of coffee (high frequency) and seldom, if ever, initiates emergency landing procedures. But if we ranked tasks by importance instead of frequency, these two tasks would be reversed.

STEPS IN CONDUCTING A TASK ANALYSIS

There is no single best way to conduct a task analysis. The method will depend upon the purpose for which the task analysis is being conducted, the nature of the job being analyzed, and the sophistication of the data required as output. There are some procedures, however, that the trainer should follow in order to assure that the data derived from the task analysis are a valid representation of the performance required for a specific job.

There are two major phases in performing a task analysis:

1. collection of the data
2. validation of the data

Collection of the Data

There are five steps that ordinarily are followed in collecting data for a task analysis, and each of these will be discussed briefly in the following paragraphs.

DEVELOPMENT OF A PRELIMINARY TASK LIST

The first step the trainer may wish to take is to collect a list of the major tasks. This can be done in any of the ways that have been discussed previously: literature search, preliminary interviews (usually with the supervisor), or direct observation.

PRELIMINARY VALIDATION

Much time and trouble will be saved if the trainer checks the validity of the task list immediately; that is, as things are mentioned in the interviews, the trainer can use direct observation, which, in the final analysis, is the most reliable means of validation. Whenever it is possible, these interviews should be conducted in the work area, since the interviewee will feel more comfortable and can point to pieces of equipment during the interview. These on-site interviews are especially helpful when the trainer is not experienced in the operation under consideration. Questions that might be overlooked in a conference room will pop up naturally in the work area. For example, the operator may talk about lifting a coupler into position. The trainer, seeing the size of the coupler, will ask, "How do you do that?" In a conference room setting, the trainer might make inaccurate assumptions about the task.

MANAGEMENT CONCURRENCE

In some cases, it may be necessary for the trainer to have the major task list reviewed by higher levels of management, especially if there is a need to get top management involved early so that they will not reject the project later. We have seen many instances in which a good deal of work had been done on a task analysis but when management finally was brought into the picture, they did not agree with the tasks listed. It is better to discover and discuss these discrepancies early to avoid difficulties later.

THE COMPLETION OF THE TASK ANALYSIS FORM

The next step is for the trainer to list all the tasks and subtasks in column 1 of the record form (Figure 3.1). By interviewing the specialists on the job and by observing the tasks being performed, the trainer can complete all the other columns on the record form. The number of columns that are used will depend upon how the data will be used: the more detailed the training program will be, the more complete the task analysis record form must be. If case studies and laboratory training sequences are planned, a much more complete task list is needed. If the trainer intends to use the task list for on-the-job training, the task list need not be as complete because some of the items such as learning difficulty, and type of performance are needed only when designing a classroom training experience.

MANAGEMENT REVIEW

Once the task analysis record form has been completed, copies of the form should be distributed to as many management personnel as possible. The more management personnel are involved at this stage of the procedure, the more cooperation the trainer will get later when the training program is conducted. Management will feel that it is their program since they helped to develop it, and the trainer will find that they will be more cooperative in allowing workers off the job to attend the training program. Once management has approved the task analysis record form, the data gathering phase of the task analysis has been completed.

Validation of the Data

By *validation* we mean that the trainer should do everything possible to make sure that the data collected on the job are an accurate description of the job. In some cases the description has been agreed upon; that is, it is the way management wants the job to be done, and the master performers in the system agree that, "Yes, the job can be done this way." In such cases it may be that the job currently is not being performed to the standard by everyone. This would be true when new equipment has been brought onto the job.

The reader will note that in the procedures outlined under collection of data, a continuing validation procedure was included. If these steps are not followed during the collection phase, it is essential that they be conducted at this point before any work in developing training objectives or training procedures is done. Failure to validate the data can lead to some very expensive training and selection errors. A classic example of this occurred with one of our clients, who was selecting salespeople based on a very simple method. When applicants came into the sales manager's office, they were handed an ashtray and told, "Sell this to me." Those applicants who were most dynamic in selling the ashtray to the sales manager were the ones who were hired. The turnover in this organization, however, was extraordinarily high. When a validation of the job analysis eventually was conducted, it was found that the job of the salesperson was primarily administrative; the salesperson had to make sure that the shelves were stocked properly and that the store managers were made aware of new products. There was no need at all for dynamic selling. Hence, the rapid turnover was a direct result of dynamic salespeople being dissatisfied with administrative work.

A SAMPLE PROCEDURE USED
TO CONDUCT A TASK ANALYSIS

Below the reader will find a recently developed procedure used to conduct a task analysis for the job of production supervisor. It is reprinted here as an example of one way of completing a task analysis.

1. Develop a plan for implementing a task analysis that identifies the steps to be completed, responsibility for completion, and completion date.
2. Review the implementation plan with the manager and the production manager to obtain concurrence.
3. Ask the production manager for the names and locations of the four best general supervisors and the six best supervisors assigned to the area.
4. Meet with the four general supervisors to explain the objective of the task analysis and implementation plan.
5. Explain how to complete the task analysis questionnaire. Distribute the form and establish a due date.
6. Have general supervisors complete questionnaires.
7. Collect the completed questionnaires.
8. Summarize the data from the questionnaires.
9. Meet individually with the general supervisors to define what, when, how well, and how often for each of the tasks identified on the task list.
10. Summarize and review the task lists with the general supervisors and the superintendent for concurrence.
11. Meet with the six supervisors to explain the objective of a task analysis. Distribute the task lists developed by the general supervisors and ask each supervisor to review the task list and add or delete any tasks as required.

12. Summarize the task lists and obtain concurrence from the area superintendent, the general supervisors, and the supervisors.
13. Meet with the six supervisors to assign procedural descriptions for each task and to develop subtasks for each task.
14. Collect the subtask descriptions and separate the data according to the task analysis record form.
15. Distribute copies of the completed task analysis to the industrial relations manager and the production manager.
16. Analyze the task analysis record form and develop abbreviated task statements and performance indicators.

SIMPLIFIED TASK ANALYSIS

There are many situations in which the trainer will not have the time or the personnel to conduct a comprehensive task analysis following the steps that we have cited. When a specific request for job training reaches the trainer, he or she may, with the assistance of the supervisor and the employee, simply list the tasks that are to be performed. This may be done informally, but it is best for the tasks and the subtasks to be put in writing. A simple method for doing this is as follows:

1. List in a logical sequence the activities involved in producing a product or a service or part thereof. This calls for a great deal of attention to detail. Do not miss any of the tasks or movements.
2. After these have been listed, question each step ruthlessly. Is each step still needed? Can it be combined with another? Can it be simplified? Under the impact of creativity of those concerned, what activity can change from time to time?
3. Ask about other tasks that happen less often, for example, once a week, once a month, or once a year. Are there emergency tasks that occur only in response to a specific situation?
4. Determine what an employee needs to know and to be able to do for each of the tasks identified.
5. Review the list with management and employees to assure accuracy and completeness.

IS TASK ANALYSIS WORTH THE TIME AND THE MONEY

In order to determine whether or not a trainer ought to conduct an extensive task analysis, a decision needs to be made about the expected outcome. In some cases, there is no question. For example, if a new piece of equipment is being brought onto the job, it is essential that some sort of task analysis be conducted. In other cases, however, the current method of training, even though it is not perfect, may be sufficient.

Prior to conducting the task analysis, the trainer ought to make a projection about anticipated benefits derived from conducting the task analysis. It may be that the amount of training time will be reduced if a good task analysis is conducted. In one case, at a trucking firm, a task analysis was conducted at a cost of about $200,000 before the first lesson unit was ever prepared.[3] The course that was eventually developed reduced the time required for training from nine weeks per person to nine days per person. This reduction in training time saved the company over $2 million a year. In other words, the course saved five times its original development cost each year, and it was offered for five years.

Although this is an unusual example of cost savings, many other less dramatic examples are available. It is only through activities like these that management will begin to see the trainer as capable of making a contribution to the bottom line of the organization. When management can see that employees are trained at less cost, that they are put on the job sooner, and so on, the training department will be treated with the same respect as other departments.

Additional Reading

1. *Handbook for Analyzing Jobs*, U.S. Department of Labor, Manpower Administration, U.S. Government Printing Office, Stock Number 2900–0131, 1972.
2. *Developing Vocational Instruction*, Mager, R. F., and Beach, K. M., Belmont, Calif.: Fearon, 1967.

---

[3] National Society for Programmed Instruction, "A Case Study of Task Analysis," *Improving Human Performance*, 2, 1 (Spring 1973): 64, 65.

Chapter 4
Writing Behavioral Objectives

"If you don't know where you're going, it doesn't matter which road you take." We believe that this statement relates to designing good classroom training programs. Before any work is done in designing the course and in developing the materials, the trainer must define the objectives of the course and have them approved by management. We also believe that any training program that is not built on a foundation of behavioral objectives must be considered suspect. In general, there are two kinds of objectives—behavioral and learning. Learning objectives are stated in terms of what the trainee will know at the end of the program; behavioral objectives are stated in terms of what the trainee will be able to do.

BEHAVIORAL OBJECTIVES

A *behavioral objective* is a statement of what the trainee will be able to do at the end of a given segment of training. Too often, trainers write the behavioral objectives from their own point of view. A behavioral objective should identify what the *trainee* will be able to *do* at the end of the training. Within this definition are several characteristics of a good objective, and these are discussed below.

Performance of the Trainees

The correctly stated behavioral objective talks about the performance of the trainees and contains a *doing* verb in it. *Note:* It does not talk about instructional material or about what the instructor will be doing.

Observable

A behavioral objective contains a doing verb that is *observable*. To say, "The trainee will understand the need for safety" is, in our opinion, a poorly written objective. A better way to write this objective would be, "The trainee will list five reasons for wearing safety glasses," or, "The trainee will recite the safety rules of the department." Note the difference between the verb "understand" and "list" or "recite"; the first is a "knowing" verb, and the second and third are "doing" verbs. Some further examples of these two types of verbs are listed below.

"Doing" verbs	*"Knowing" verbs*
say	understand
count	appreciate
place	develop an attitude for
point out	see the value of
install	increase
complete	grow
fix	recognize
replace	
solve	

Conditions

A behavioral objective defines the important *conditions* under which the behavior is going to occur. These conditions answer one or both of these questions, "What are the givens?" or "What are the restrictions?" For example, in some cases the trainee will have to perform from memory. In such a case the behavioral objective would read, "Working from memory the trainee will tell. . . ." In other cases, the trainee will be given a job aid. (An example of a job aid might be a chart used by an employee in a chemical plant to determine the proper mix of the raw materials.) In the training program, the trainee's objective will be stated in these terms: "Given the chart that outlines the proper mixes of raw material, the trainee will describe the appropriate blends for the following compounds. . . ." It may include the tools or equipment used, for example, "Given the lathe and a piece of bar stock . . ." or "Given seven application forms, the trainee will identify those that are incorrectly completed."

Standards

A behavioral objective defines the standards of acceptable performance, for example, "three out of four correct," "all of the time," "with four out of five shots in the target," "with fewer than two errors," "with a tolerance of plus or minus 10," and so on.

LEARNING OBJECTIVES

The objectives we have discussed are *terminal;* that is, they define a behavior a trainee will be able to perform at the conclusion of a unit or perhaps an entire program. Often there are subobjectives that are important for the trainer to know and understand in developing and designing a training course. These are called *intermediate* or *learning objectives.*

A question the trainer should ask while building a module around a terminal behavioral objective is this: "What does a trainee need to *know* in order to perform this terminal objective?" For example, in order to complete a sales transaction, the trainee needs to know how to add (and how to multiply if there happens to be a sales tax). Knowing how to add and how to multiply are intermediate learning objectives that lead to the terminal behavioral objective of completing a sales transaction.

OBTAINING MANAGEMENT COMMITMENT

No manager would buy a piece of equipment and install it without knowing *exactly* what that piece of equipment is going to be able to do, how it is going to perform, and what effect it is going to have on the organization. We feel the same ought to be true of training programs that managers are expected to buy. They have the right to be given specific objectives stated in terms of what employees will be able to do when they leave the training program and return to the job.

Behavioral objectives, when they are properly written, are a very powerful tool for the trainer to use in obtaining management's commitment to the training program. After the needs analysis has been completed and shared with management, the trainer should establish a list of behavioral objectives for the training program and share those objectives with management. A statement such as this should be made: "Mr./Ms. X, are these the things you want your people to be able to do? If so, we can design a training program that will train them to be able to do these things. The cost of the training program will be $x." If the manager says, "Yes, that's exactly what I want my people to be able to do. They need to be able to do these things in order to perform on their jobs or to overcome the problems we have been experiencing," then the trainer will have management's commitment. Now all that is left for the trainer to do is deliver the changed behavior.

When trainers do not go through this step, they should not then wonder why managers reject their training programs. If the managers understand what it is they are going to get out of the program, they are less likely to reject the program just because money is tight. Furthermore, properly designed and accepted objectives form a "road map" for designing the training program.

TAXONOMY FOR INSTRUCTIONAL OBJECTIVES

Trainers who are serious about writing good behavioral objectives (those in programmed instruction, for example) should become acquainted with Bloom's Taxonomy.[1] The first volume, developed in 1956, is concerned specifically with the cognitive areas of training. It divides the cognitive domain into six categories, all of which relate to the recall or recognition of knowledge and the development of intellectual abilities. These six categories are:

recall
comprehension
application
analysis
synthesis
evaluation

The lowest-order objective consists of straight recall or recognition; that is, a student shows that he or she can repeat the facts,

[1] Benjamin S. Bloom et al. (Ed.), *Taxonomy of Educational Objectives* (New York: David McKay Company, Inc., 1956).

use the terminology, and so forth. Bloom lists an extraordinary number of "doing" verbs that fit into this category.

At the other end of the list are those "doing" verbs that confirm the student's ability to evaluate knowledge. This area is much more difficult than simple recall because it requires an agreement on the criteria involved in making a "good evaluation." Here also Bloom lists a large number of "doing" verbs with subcategories to help the trainer write good behavioral objectives in the cognitive domain.

In 1958 Bloom and his associates published a second taxonomy covering the affective domain, that is, interests, attitudes, values, development of appreciation, and adequate personal adjustment. It is, of course, difficult to assess the progress of participants using these dimensions, but they can be significant and valid terminal objectives.

Many trainers feel that these taxonomies are unnecessary for most industrial training programs. In our training experience, for example, we have found we rarely needed the nuances Bloom provides to describe adequately the terminal objectives we wanted for our industrial trainees. Those who are concentrating in instructional technology, however, and are working in programmed instruction, will find these taxonomies essential.

HOW TO WRITE BEHAVIORAL OBJECTIVES

It is relatively easy to write good training objectives if the trainer follows a few simple steps and keeps in mind that the descriptions concern what the trainees will be able to *do* at the end of the training segment, the conditions under which they will have to perform, and the criteria for success.

The following are the steps the trainer should use in writing behavioral objectives:

1. Write out the *job or task* that is going to be done. At first use only a verb and a noun. For example:
   a. Identify counterfeit $10 bills.
   b. Conduct a disciplinary hearing.
   c. Point out the pinch points on the duplicating machine.
2. Add the *quantity standards* or criteria that are going to be applied to the behavioral objective. For example:
   a. Identify *18* counterfeit $10 bills *from a stack of 20.*
   b. Conduct *one* disciplinary hearing.
   c. Point out the *seven* pinch points on the duplicating machine.

3. Add the *quality criteria* that will be included in the behavioral objective. For example:
   a. Identify the 18 counterfeit $10 bills from a stack of 20 *with no more than one error.*
   b. Conduct one disciplinary hearing *without violating any clauses of the labor agreement.*
   c. Point out the seven pinch points on the duplicating machine. (Note that in the absence of a quality standard statement the quality is assumed to be 100 percent. In this last statement, all seven of the pinch points must be identified.)
4. Add the *circumstances,* that is, the tools and equipment with which the trainees will be performing the objective. For example:
   a. *Given twenty* $10 bills, identify the 18 counterfeit bills with only one error.
   b. *Given a case study involving an employee who has been absent on the job repeatedly,* conduct a disciplinary hearing without violating any of the labor agreement rules.
   c. *Given a duplicating machine operating normally and a diagram of that machine,* point out the seven pinch points.

CONCLUSION

The use of behavioral objectives in designing a training program serves a number of valuable purposes for the trainer. Behavioral objectives provide input for evaluation, help avoid training that focuses on impractical theories, and provide tests for validating training processes. Trainers should be careful to be honest in developing behavioral objectives. They are helpful only if they are real, relevant, and measurable at the conclusion of the training.

Additional Reading

1. *Taxonomy of Educational Objectives,* Bloom, Benjamin S. et al. (Ed.), New York: McKay, Cognitive Domain—1956; Affective Domain—1964.
2. *Setting Precise Performance Objectives,* Wilson, V., Princeton, N.J.: Brandon/Systems Press, 1969.
3. *Measuring Instructional Intent,* Mager, R. F., Belmont, Calif.: Fearon, 1973.
4. *Preparing Instructional Objectives,* Mager, R. F., Belmont, Calif.: Fearon, 1962.

Chapter 5
Designing
Effective Training

HOW ADULTS LEARN

The term "andragogy" is beginning to be used regularly in training literature despite the fact that it is not listed in Webster's. It is generally used to differentiate how adults learn from how children learn (called "pedagogy"). This distinction is not precisely accurate although it is a helpful start. We prefer to define these terms differently. Pedagogy is the process in which information is transmitted from a teacher to a student, with the teacher assuming full responsibility for what, when, how, and to whom the information is taught. Much of our elementary, secondary, and even college education is pedagogy. Teaching children the multiplication tables and teaching essential job procedures to new employees are examples. Some pedagogical characteristics are listed:

There is a "right" answer.
The teacher decides the content.
Rote memory is commonly used by the student.
The student lacks experience.
The need for learning is dictated by the teacher.

The teacher is the source of wisdom.

The teacher evaluates the progress of the student.

The material is new to the student.

The need for learning the material is delayed rather than immediate.

Lecture, demonstration, and practice are commonly used teaching techniques.

Attendance is usually mandated.

Andragogy is a learning process in which both the student and the teacher assume responsibility for what, when, how, and to whom information is taught. Some characteristics of andragogy follow:

The student accepts the content based on evidence, not blind faith.

The student is active rather than passive.

The student has experience in the subject and brings that experience into the classroom.

The student has individual needs that must be addressed.

The student evaluates himself or herself.

Immediate application of the concepts is common.

Discussion and experimentation are commonly used teaching methods.

Attendance is often optional.

An example of andragogy is the way we conduct management training. We work under the assumption that every member of the class knows how to communicate properly with another person; that is, each person understands on an intellectual level how to get a message across. As a matter of fact, the members of the class all demonstrate this ability daily in their families, in their churches, and in their community life. Yet, it seems that when they are given the title "supervisor," some of them are unable to apply these principles of good communication. We see our job as facilitators—helping trainees to identify those principles of communication that they already know and to turn them into behaviors that they can apply on the job.

There is a basic principle of motivation drawn from management literature that applies to the classroom as much as it does to the job: "If hard work leads to success, and success leads to recognition, and recognition leads to valued rewards, you then have a motivated worker." This same principle applies in the classroom. If the adult student sees that effort expended in the classroom will lead to learning, that learning will lead to an application of the concepts to the job, that application will lead to success, and that recognition of that success and subsequent reward will follow, then, we will have a motivated student.

The more students participate in the training situation, the greater its effectiveness and the longer the students' retention will be. Unless the adult students have been involved in the training, they will tend not to internalize the concepts learned in the training program, and therefore, will not transfer their classroom learning to on-the-job situations.

AN EXPERIENTIAL LEARNING MODEL

In order to develop fully the participatory and discovery learning process, we recommend that trainers use the following learning design model, as shown in Figure 5.1. This model can be used in the development of any training program. The following paragraphs will explain in detail each subsection of the model.

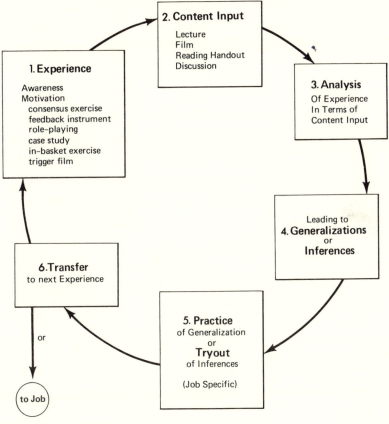

Figure 5.1   Learning Model

1. Experience

Each training or learning unit begins with an *experience;* the trainer has the trainees *do* something. This has a distinct value because the trainees will have increased their motivation for learning before they receive the *content input.* This awareness experience helps to avoid the "sermon syndrome." (The sermon syndrome develops when a person hears a sermon and thinks, "Hey, that's really a terrific idea. I hope my wife/husband is listening to this because it really applies to him/her." The person hears some good ideas and then says, "Right on, that's just what I'm doing.") Requiring the trainees to have an experience within the area of the content input will increase their opportunity for becoming aware of how they currently handle related situations. They will also gain an understanding of the needs for the material that follows.

This initial experiential exercise should emphasize *process.* It should require the trainees to become involved in situations entailing the same skills, processes, ideas, or attitudes that will be developed in the learning session or skill session that will follow. One word of caution is necessary here. This opening exercise should not guarantee failure. Trainers often put trainees in situations in which the skills being tested cannot be accomplished given the entry skill level of the class. This supposedly proves how badly the training program is needed, but in reality only destroys motivation.

We feel that this first experience need not be related specifically to the trainees' jobs; it ought to be general in its approach. This helps avoid the problem of trainees discounting the exercise and the awareness they should have obtained and saying, "In my department, we wouldn't have done it that way" or, "In our area, our manager doesn't let us. . . ."

Here are two examples of exercises that are not job specific. A training program in negotiating, coaching, or counseling might use a role playing exercise that involves a parent and child in some form of negotiation. The sixteen-year-old would like to have access to the family car. The parent would like to have certain chores done on a regular basis. Or, a training program on interviewing skills might use an exercise in which the trainees actually interview each other as a part of the introductions. We have used an exercise in which one trainee assumes the role of a scout executive who is interviewing a classmate for the position of scout master. This experience vividly points out a trainee's tendency to ask irrelevant questions in determining qualifications for a job. It allows for an analysis of real behavior so that all trainees can become aware of the kinds of questions that they should ask in an interview: they will often see that they ask leading rather than nonleading questions, and they will learn to judge how well they have listened or whether they have used follow-up questions to probe for more information.

There are a variety of situations, exercises, or simulations that the trainer can use to develop this initial experience, a few of which we will discuss below. (Later in this chapter we will discuss various involvement techniques thoroughly.)

GAMES

There are numerous training games of short time spans. (This is not the time to use longer or more complex games such as computer games or simulations. These belong in the practice sessions that will be described later.) Numerous books and catalogs of these games are available to the trainer who is designing a program. (Some of them are listed in the Additional Reading section at the end of this chapter.)

PRETESTS

Pretests may be used in a number of ways. They may serve as an awareness exercise by testing the trainee's entry knowledge or skill level. They also may be used to plan a particular learning map, so that all trainees will not have to go through everything if they already know some of the answers. Pretests may also serve as an evaluation tool to test learning. Through administration of a post-test, which may be identical or similar to the pretest, the amount of learning can be measured.

INSTRUMENTED FEEDBACK

Using paper and pencils, the trainees (often both supervisors and subordinates) respond to situations and describe how they would handle administrative problems. Numerous resources for obtaining these exercises are available.

2. Content Input

The next step in our training model (see Figure 5.1) is for the trainer to give a brief *content input* to the participants, (that is, the material or concepts to be taught). We use the word "brief" intentionally, because we feel that many trainers spend too much time delivering content. The trainees do not need to know everything about Maslow[1] or Herzberg[2] or McClelland[3] in order to make decisions about how to motivate employees. (Some would argue that the trainees need to know nothing about the theorists—and indeed, this may be true—but we prefer to provide some education along with the training.)

The role of the content input is to give the trainees a model against which they can analyze their on-the-job behavior and training experiences. The objective of the content input is *not* just to teach concepts to the trainees; knowing something, in and of itself, will not improve performance on the job.

There are many techniques that can be used for content input. The most obvious of these is the lecture, or the *lecturette*. (Consistent use of the term *lecturette* will help to remind trainers that content input ought to be brief.) We are convinced that the trainees will enjoy the lecture and learn more when the trainer avoids the academic proclivity of naming names, text references, and dates. These are usually totally irrelevant to performance on the job. If credibility is needed, it may be provided by handing out articles that approach the academics of the content. Other techniques that can be used for content input are films, reading resources, and group discussions.

A common mistake many trainers make is to assume that the content input is the most important part of the training process; it is not. It is a necessary part, but it is only one part of the total process. The trainees need a model against which to analyze their behavior, but learning that model is not the most important part of the process.

We ought to say a word here about behavior modeling which is a training design that recently has been used more and more. We feel a basic concern about the use of modeling as a training tool. (This concern underlies our reason for putting the experience first and the content input second.) Under the modeling system, the content input is given first; that is, the correct model is given first. Then the trainees are placed in a situation in which they attempt to "model" their behavior to the content input just given. We believe that one could watch a piece of film depicting how a manager should handle a discipline problem and mimic the behavior of the person on the film exactly. Yet despite this, the trainees can leave the train-

[1] A. H. Maslow, "A Theory of Human Motivation," *Psychological Review,* 50 (1943): 370–396.
[2] Frederick Herzberg, Bernard Mausner, and Barbara Bloch Synderman, *The Motivation to Work* (New York: Wiley, 1959).
[3] D. C. McClelland et al., *The Achievement Motive* (Englewood Cliffs, N.J.: Prentice-Hall, 1961).

ing program without ever having recognized that they need to change their behavior on the job; the *awareness* is missing. The motivation for change rests with the trainer, not with the trainee. The use of modeling works well in situations in which the trainees have no idea how to perform given tasks.

3. Analysis

The third step in the training model (see Figure 5.1) is to have the trainees analyze the experience they had (Step 1) against the content input (Step 2). It is best to let the trainees do their own analysis. If the awareness was created in an individual setting, the options of individual analysis, small group analysis, or team analysis should be considered. After a small group analysis, the trainer should bring all the trainees together for a debriefing.

It is very helpful for the trainees to have some kind of guidance in doing this analysis such as a set of questions to be answered about the experience, for example: "What body language cues did you see?" "What else could have been done?" "How did the supervisor in the role playing respond to the challenge by the subordinate?" "What went wrong?" "What would you have done?" or "What would you do next?" With questions such as these, the trainees can do an effective analysis without input or interference from the trainer.

4. Generalizations or Inferences

The next step in the training model (see Figure 5.1) is for the trainees, as individuals or as a group, to draw generalizations or inferences based on the analysis just completed. The difference between a *generalization* and an *inference* is that a generalization is a fact that a person can accept immediately and act on, whereas an inference is a rule that a person can accept tentatively but that needs to be tested before the person is willing to incorporate it into his or her behavior. The following are two examples of generalizations or inferences that a group might draw:

> In a communications training program the group, after analyzing the way they have responded to some conflict situations, may draw as a generalization or inference that in problem-solving situations, managers are more likely to succeed if they are able to maintain a problem-solving posture rather than jump at quick solutions.

In an interviewing training program, the group may draw as a generalization or inference that better information can be obtained about the interviewee when open-ended questions are asked rather than when leading questions are asked.

5. Practice or Tryout

After generalizations or inferences have been drawn, the next step is for the trainees to practice using the generalizations or to test (try out) the inferences (see Figure 5.1). This practice or tryout is often very similar to the experience in the Step 1 of the training model. Unlike the first experience, however, the practice or tryout *must be job related* or job specific. Once the trainees have drawn a generalization about a behavior, they should practice that behavior in a situation as joblike as possible. If they are testing an inference, they should try it out in a setting very much like the one on the job. When the results are determined, they will have confidence that the rule will work on the job.

The following are two examples of the practice or tryout:

Participants develop role playing situations from things that happen on their jobs and in this way test the generalization or inference. For example, in a communications workshop the trainees identify situations in which a supervisor inappropriately talked down to an employee. Then the trainees role-play to handle these real life situations.

In an interpersonal skills training program for first-line supervisors, we have often enlisted the services of second- and third-line supervisors in the organization to role-play an hourly employee. After the first-line supervisors have learned some rules for improving interpersonal skills, they are presented with conflict situations that have been identified in the needs analysis as difficult ones to handle. They have a chance to actually try out the new rules. By using the second- and third-line supervisors as employees in the tryout, a distinct touch of realism is added.

6. Transfer

The last step in the training model (see Figure 5.1) is for the trainer to *transfer* or assist the trainees in using the knowledge or skills once they return to their jobs. It is sometimes uncomfortable to take the trainees through this transfer process, because it may seem parental and overly directive. We must conclude, however, that no matter how enthused the trainees are at the end of a training program, there is a need for some formal transference of the training to the job situations. Trainees need to work through an exercise that will facilitate this transfer.

In Chapter 8 we discuss some specific techniques a trainer can and should use to assist trainees in transferring the things learned in the classroom into practice on the job.

BASIC FACTORS TO CONSIDER IN DESIGNING TRAINING PROGRAMS

Every instructional strategy has certain advantages and limitations. Careful consideration should be given to the advantages and limitations of each to ensure that the strategy selected for a specific program will be effective. Design decisions must be made based on an analysis of the training situation from several points of view: the instructional objectives, the course content, the student population and class size, the instructors, the facilities, the equipment and materials, the time available, and the costs.

Instructional Objectives

The primary consideration in determining the techniques and strategies to be used in a training program is, "What will the trainee be required to do at the end of the program or at a later stage in the course?" It is apparent that a program or a module of a program whose objective is to build concepts will require different interaction and training strategies than one that will teach manual skills.

Course Content

The nature of the content must be considered when the trainer selects an instructional strategy, for example, "Is the content verbal or manipulative?" "Is the content difficult?" or "How new is the content to the experiences of the trainees?"

Student Population and Class Size

Size, prior training, aptitudes, learning capacity, maturity, and reading and speaking ability of the group all must be considered in selecting a training strategy. Classes may have as few as 5 trainees or as many as 300. When a client asks how many employees we can accommodate in a class, our answer is, "as many as is necessary." The trainer should design the program to fit the number of trainees and should not assume that the same method of instruction or presentation will be appropriate for all groups. This is a major weakness of many "packaged" programs.

Instructors

The number of instructors available and their competencies and weaknesses are important factors in considering a strategy. For example, if the decision has been made to bring in trainers from the line management group, the design of the program must be one that does not require strong platform speaking experience, since many of the line supervisors will not have this experience. On the other hand, discussions about what happens on the job would be an appropriate instructional technique.

Facilities

Under ideal conditions the trainer chooses the facilities to support the instructional strategy and techniques developed for the program. In some situations, however, the reverse is true. In many organizations the training facilities become a deciding factor in determining the training strategy. For example, a lack of space for several rooms may dictate against trying to tape team discussions for replaying later.

Equipment and Materials

Under normal conditions the equipment and instructional materials should be chosen to support the instructional design of the program; however, it is quite conceivable that the reverse will be true. The trainer may have restrictions imposed, in terms of audiovisual equipment, for example, and so the instructional strategy will have to fit the equipment available. In other cases major investments in hardware (videotape, for example) may dictate the use of equipment whether or not it is appropriate.

Time

The time available for a particular module of instruction will often govern the strategy selected. Consensus technique is a time-consuming process if it is to be done right. If only a block of time of less than two hours is available, a different technique is required, or prework may be assigned.

Costs

The question of cost is a very practical one in any training program. When a client asks, "Can you do such and such?," our answer is, "We can do anything you want if you are willing to bear the cost." If some needs analysis has been done and some cost/value analysis has been completed, decisions about the cost effectiveness of the training program can be made readily.

MATCHING DESIGN TO TYPE OF PERFORMANCE

Many trainers have a method of instruction that they feel most comfortable using, and when they design a training program, they use this favored procedure. For example, some are better lecturers than discussion leaders, and others like to use slides and discussion. Professional trainers look at more than just what they feel comfortable with when they design a training program. They will choose their tools in the same way that a master carpenter does: they first will decide what needs to be accomplished and then will choose an instructional procedure that will best accomplish the objective.

There are several different kinds of performance, and different instructional procedures and materials are appropriate for each. For example, role-playing and discussion might be excellent for teaching interviewing techniques but not for teaching someone how to run a lathe. This is obvious, but why? The answer is that there are two different kinds of performance involved: in one case we are talking about speech and in the other case we are talking about manipulation.

The information on the following pages may help the trainer in planning training designs.

Discrimination

Discrimination between objects or between what is and what ought to be can be taught by showing the trainees pairs of things in which they need to see a difference. Once the trainees are able to identify the difference between the two items, then the trainer shows them just one item and asks them to identify whether or not this item fits the mental image of the way it ought to be.

In teaching trainees how to identify counterfeit $20 bills, they would be shown a number of counterfeit bills, all of which have the same distinguishing characteristic that makes them counterfeit. Once the trainees are able to remember and point out this characteristic, they would be given a stack with both counterfeit and non-counterfeit bills to identify which ones have this counterfeit characteristic. The trainees should be given immediate knowledge of the results to correct their mental images.

Trainees must have practice sessions when the objective of the training is discrimination, for example, being able to tell whether a job has been done properly, whether a job needs to be done, or the difference between a proper and improper way of doing a job. It does not help if they just talk about it; discussion is not related to doing the task. Lectures and discussions are used to give the trainees criteria for discriminating, but if the trainer wants to make sure that trainees can actually perform, they must practice discrimination in realistic simulations.

Problem Solving

Problem solving is best taught by

showing the trainees cues or symptoms that will lead them to recognize that some sort of problem solving is called for

showing the relationships between the symptoms and the possible causes

giving practice on the actual apparatus or on the actual symptoms and letting trainees solve the problem.

Once again, problem solving is not taught by lecturing about it or by having the trainees write about it, talk about it, or answer multiple choice questions about it. Problem solving is a skill and not a knowledge.

A good example of teaching problem solving can be seen in electrical training. The trainee is shown an instrument that is not operating properly. After the trainee discriminates that, in fact, the instrument is not operating properly, he or she then needs to identify the possible causes of the improper operation. The trainee may be taught that the first step is to check the circuits because 90 percent of the time that is where the problem is or to check the input and the output of electricity in the various components to determine if there is an unusual drop in voltage and to determine where that drop occurs. After having learned these techniques, the trainee is shown actual instruments with built-in malfunctions. He or she then tries to identify the cause of the problem and to apply the proper remedy.

Recall

The techniques used to teach recall depend on the kind of performance desired. If the trainees need to recall a specific procedure, then a combination of lecture and demonstration followed by practice probably is appropriate. If the task is to identify the names of various objects, the training can sometimes be conducted quite successfully by showing pictures of the objects and telling their names and then mixing up the pictures so that the trainees must identify the names of each of the objects. It is better, however, to show the trainees the real objects instead of pictures of the objects, since the transfer of training from the classroom to the job is easier when real objects are used.

If pictures are used, the trainer should take the picture in its proper setting. If the trainees learn to recognize a valve control in an isolated close-up color photo but then find the location of the valve on the job to be hidden underneath a control box, covered with grease, good recall is much less likely.

In many cases when a procedure needs to be recalled, a job aid will be the most appropriate training method. Rather than require the trainees to remember a difficult and complicated procedure, the trainer should teach the trainees to understand how to use the job aid, which fully explains the procedure. The job aid should be permanently and prominently displayed at the work location. One of the best examples of this was developed at Michigan State University for the paramedics in Lansing. The paramedics were given a "blue sheet" that listed the procedure to follow when they found a person lying on the street or on the ground. The first step was to identify if the person was breathing. If the person was breathing, the paramedic would move to the second step, which called for another discrimination, and so on. (If the person was not breathing, the sequence ended quickly.)

Speech

The principal technique for teaching specific speech characteristics involves content input followed by a testing or a tryout and some immediate knowledge of the results. Feedback conducted by peers or instructors is indispensable. The best feedback occurs when the trainees are able to *see* the results of the way they have said something. In such cases a tape recorder (either video or audio) is an excellent tool, because it allows the trainees to actually see or hear what worked or what did not work and why.

INTERACTION TECHNIQUES

When designing training programs, particularly those aimed at interpersonal skills development, the trainer must design the program so that the trainees are involved in the learning process. There are many interaction models that can do this: games, force-field analysis, discussions, consensus discussion groups, role playing, trigger films, and instrumented feedback.

Games

Games are often used successfully in interpersonal skill training programs. (Usually the word "experience" or "exercise" rather than "game" is used in order to reduce the chance of turning off the trainees; "What are we doing here playing silly games?") The games or experiential learning exercises fit best as the initial experience in the training model. When people get involved in a game (i.e., when people are trying to solve a puzzle, to communicate, to make a decision, to identify a problem, or whatever is involved in the game), their behavior is characteristic of their behavior when they are involved in similar activities on the job. Because of this, games provide trainees with real data to analyze in the training program.

A very important warning must be made about games. Too many trainers obtain a series of books or exercises from catalogues and put together a training program that consists of one experiential learning game after another. They open the book and say, "Let's see, number 7, 14, 23, and 54. Good! Now, I've got a training program." This is not how a training program should be designed. One of the rules we follow is to use only one "exotic" game in a one-day program and only two or three games in a week-long interpersonal program. Games should be used only if they provide meaningful support to the specific learning objective.

The most essential part of a game is the debriefing, that is, the analysis of what happened so that trainees can draw their generalizations and inferences. The debriefing is generally led by a trainer, but it is important that the trainer work as a catalyst rather than as a dictator in the debriefing.

There are two commonly used techniques for beginning the debriefing. In the first technique the trainer might ask, "What was the exercise all about?" Then the trainer would hold a brainstorming session in which the trainees would name all the different things they thought the exercise was about. These would be listed on a flip chart. Once these ideas are posted, the group can go over the flip chart using the input as a discussion outline.

For example, we frequently use "The Aggressive Corporation," a highly competitive, zero-sum game aimed at teaching the pros and cons of cooperation and competition.[4] We typically get answers like these when we asked what the game was about:

strategy
trust
communication
competition
winning
convincing others to do something
"beat your buddy"
not listening

With the second technique the trainer would throw a question out to the group for discussion. The question might be, "OK, what happened during the exercise?" The trainer would then lead a discussion, drawing from the trainees the thoughts and feelings they had during the game. It is sometimes necessary for the trainer to call upon one of the trainees to get his or her perception of what another trainee is saying. For example, if one of the trainees, in answer to the original question says, "I really felt good when I explained my idea to the group and they all agreed with me," the trainer might turn to the rest of the group and ask, "Did everyone here agree with her?" If some of the trainees say, "No, we really didn't agree with her at that point," the first trainee should be assisted in order to see the positive and negative aspects of what she did during the game.

Whenever a game is used in a training program, the trainer should take notes of various occurrences that will be discussed during the debriefing. If an item noted comes up in a discussion, the trainer can simply cross it off the list. If the trainer notes something that none of the trainees have mentioned, then he or she can bring it up for discussion.

[4] "The Aggressive Corporation" by Ron Kregoski, published by Consulting Associates, 1977.

Sometimes, trainers feel uneasy about directly confronting trainees about their behavior in an experiential learning situation, but if the trainees are properly prepared at the beginning of the program and at the beginning of each exercise, problems can be avoided. By preparing the participants properly we mean setting the ground rules under which the exercise will operate. Such statements as the following can be made: "This is a learning laboratory where you have a chance to experiment with various kinds of behaviors to find out what happens. Just as in any physical laboratory, we sometimes learn more from our mistakes and failures than we do from our successes. You will often find that when you analyze something that does not work, you will learn how to be more effective on the job. There are going to be times when, in order to facilitate that learning, we will put the spotlight on individuals here in the class. Our intention is not to embarrass you or to make you feel uncomfortable but rather to highlight some specific behavior so that we can all learn from the activity."

Force-field Analysis

Force-field analysis, which was described in Chapter 2, can also be used as an interactive or participative model in the classroom. One education consultant we know uses the force-field analysis to conduct day-and-a-half programs for school districts in the Michigan area. He brings together the participants on Friday after classes and begins the session by having the participants develop force-field analyses on the effectiveness of education within the school system. After the participants have completed that process, they go to dinner while the consultant and his staff use the force-field analyses data to develop a list of problems in the system. After dinner the participants work in small groups to identify the top 10 problems on the list. The next day is spent with the participants working on solutions to the problems identified as most important.

Discussions

Discussions are one of the most time honored interactive models. These discussions can be used in a number of places in the training model. They lend themselves especially to the transfer, analysis, and generalization sections of the training model. Through the use of discussion, the trainees can learn from their peers. Usually this kind of learning is far more acceptable than if it were presented in lectures by the trainer.

Consensus Discussion Groups

The consensus discussion group is an excellent technique for getting participation in a training program. It is so powerful and has so many uses that we almost always include it in some form in the training programs that we conduct. It is especially valuable for getting trainees to consider alternative strategies for handling certain problems, to discuss various attitudes among fellow workers, and to discuss priorities that differ.

The first step in the consensus technique is for the trainer to have each individual make a decision on something, for example, agreeing or disagreeing with a list of statements, ranking a list of items, picking the 10 most important items from a list of 25 items, handling an in-basket item, and so forth. It is essential that the trainees *write* their choices.

In the second step the trainees meet in small groups (of five or six preferably) and work toward achieving a group answer to the same set of questions, statements, or lists. Then the teams present their results to the rest of the group. This usually can be done quickly if the teams write their answers on a previously prepared flip chart.

The next step is for the group to discuss the questions or statements, noting both agreement and disagreement. The purpose of this discussion (debriefing) is not to achieve a consensus of the entire group but to make sure that all sides of the issues have been discussed. At this point, if there is a "correct answer" or a "book answer," the trainer shares it with the trainees. This serves as the content input portion of the training model. (The consensus discussion serves as the experience portion of the model.) The trainees then continue by comparing their original opinions against the answers given.

The consensus technique can be used for both content and process training. Some examples of using the consensus technique for content input are these:

> Begin the session by having the trainees work the consensus model with a list of 10 statements about training, management, communications, values, and so forth. These statements should represent the general areas that will be covered in the rest of the training program. Thus, this exercise serves as an introduction to the content of the program.
>
> In a management skills program, have teams identify which of 25 managerial skills are the 10 most important. After each

team makes its choices, the pros and cons of each of the 25 items should be discussed. *Note:* In an exercise like this, there is no correct answer. However, it provides an opportunity for trainees and trainer alike to comment on various aspects of management.

In a parent-teenager program, tell the parents to try to rank order a set of values, predicting what their children did in an earlier session. By sharing the actual answers of the teenagers, effective discussion among the parents and the teenagers about the differences in the way they see values will result.

When the consensus technique for process training is used, there are a few points the trainer should keep in mind.

In order to make it easier for the trainees to focus on "process" in interpersonal training, use a noncontent consensus exercise. A noncontent exercise is one in which the content is of no real value to the trainees. This keeps them from using "We-do-not-do-it-this-way-in-our-department" ploys to avoid examining processes.

When you conduct a consensus exercise aimed at process, always record, either on videotape or on audiotape, the small group portion of the exercise. In this way, after the correct answer or the book answer has been given to the trainees and after the data have been analyzed, each group can go back to its own conference room and listen to the tape. The feedback we have received from trainees has been overwhelmingly positive about this technique. They have reported that they did not realize how much they interrupted, hopped from subject to subject, communicated poorly, and how quickly they jumped to conclusions without analyzing problems.

Role-Playing and Situational Playing

Most trainers somewhere have participated in a role-playing exercise. We have some negative thoughts about the value of many role-playing situations, because sometimes the trainees are placed in unreal situations or situations to which they cannot relate. For example, a 43-year-old male, who is married and has three children, may be required in a role-playing situation to pretend to be a 23-year-old single woman. Too much time is spent trying to be the person, and this is distracting to the purpose of the role-playing.

As an alternative, better results occur with *situational playing.*

In situational playing, the trainees are themselves; they are given situations that they will play out. For example, one of the trainees has been called in by his boss and told that "Because of a special project I'm giving you, you are going to have to cancel your vacation plans" or another trainee is asked to face a customer who says, "The shipment you promised has not arrived." They do not have to pretend to be anyone else; they are themselves, and they act as they really would in that kind of situation.

Situational playing tends to be most effective when the two participants are given similar information with interesting twists. For example:

> The trainee in the first situation already has changed vacation plans twice and has promised his family a trip to a family reunion scheduled during this time.
> In the second situation, the trainee frequently has broken promises before and the customer does not want to believe her.

Or, in a different situation,

> The first trainee in the situation may be given information that he is a good employee, in fact, one of the better employees in the department. He works long hours and often puts in casual overtime without pay just to make sure that the job gets done. The boss, on the other hand, has been given slightly different information. The employee is one of the better employees, but recently his work has been slipping. Specifically, the employee has been taking longer and longer lunch hours and the boss is concerned that this might be the beginning of a down-turn in his performance. Also, the boss is concerned about the effect on the other people in the department. In this situation the trainees taking the part of the boss and the employee can be themselves.

The situation can be conducted in front of the class and critiqued by the class or the situation can be conducted in a closed room with a tape recorder running (the latter often is preferred). After the situation has concluded, the class critiques it. In either case the trainees should be given guidelines to follow in critiquing. This may consist of a list of questions to be answered or a list of things for them to look for while they are watching or listening to the situational playing. A good rule is to let the role players critique their own behavior first, and then let the observers make comments. This reduces the defensiveness of the role players.

Often role-playing or situational playing is used to provide the players a chance to experience and practice a technique for their own learning. Do not underestimate the opportunities for learning, analysis, modeling, and self-projection the player gets. In many of these situations, the greatest learning will come from observing others.

Trigger Films

One technique that is very successful for promoting interaction among trainees is called *trigger films*. A trigger film is not intended to teach. It is a very brief (often only two to four minutes) slice of life to which the participants react. For example, they may be required to state what they would say next in a situation, they may be required to determine what one of the people in the film should have done, or they may be required to identify errors.

Use of trigger films can be combined with the consensus technique very effectively. The trainees individually answer the question, "What would you say next if you were the boss in the film?" and then work in small teams to answer the same question.

Good trigger films are difficult to locate. Most films are scripted, often artificial, stilted, and even comical. Rule number one for identifying good trigger films is, do not overemphasize quality. High emphasis on flashy cameras, lighting, studio effects does not add, and often destroys a sense of realism.

A second rule is to avoid scripted situations. You may wish to produce your own triggers. The easiest and most effective way is to give the participants situations, and then videotape the interaction. You will not use all the tape you get—only the best two or three minutes.

When taping or filming, try to get out of the players' way, preferably into another room. Amateurs have trouble acting naturally if directors, camera operators, observers, training types, or supervisors are standing around and watching. For realism, try to work on the site, on the line, in the office, or in the hall. This greatly increases the credibility and realism of the film.

Instrumented Feedback

Instrumented feedback is a written questionnaire or survey that the trainer gives to trainees and others on the job for completing. Depending on the nature of the program, the people on the job may be peers, subordinates, or supervisors. For example, in a management skills program an instrument that measures the style a manager uses is completed by the manager and by two or three subordinates of the manager as prework to the workshop. This serves as the first experience in the training model. In the workshop the trainees are given the content input of the managerial concept and then asked to score the feedback instruments. The discussion and analysis that follow focus on the similarities and differences between the perceptions of the manager and his or her subordinates.

Instrumented feedback is a particularly powerful device, because it brings feedback from on the job in a form that is not threatening to either the managers or the subordinates.

CONTENT INPUT TECHNIQUES

Lecture

The lecture is the most common technique of content input. It is basically a means of providing trainees with information they need to know. Lectures can be more effective if they are interspersed with other instructional techniques such as discussion, audiovisual aids, creative overhead slides or flip charts.

Some of the problems of the lecture technique are:

It involves primarily one-way communication.
It requires a teaching skill that some trainers do not have.
It appeals mainly to only one of the senses of the participants.
It puts the participants in a passive situation.

Conference Method

The conference method is one in which group discussion techniques are used to communicate the content input. The discussion is directed either by the trainer or by written discussion guidelines.

Some of the problems of the conference method are:

It requires highly skilled trainers to keep the discussion focused.
It consumes considerably more time than does the lecture method.
It restricts the size of the group. (There has been some research showing that the conference method should not be used with groups larger than 12 to 15 participants because the opportunity for individual participation becomes too limited.)

Films

Films and videotapes are often excellent content input techniques. One of the mistakes inexperienced trainers often make is to see the film or the videotape as a total package and not recognize that there is no need to show the entire film.

One major advantage of films or videotapes is that they often are an inexpensive way of getting the message of a recognized expert. Many outstanding films are available in which some of the most expensive, most difficult to schedule, or even deceased experts are able to deliver their messages for the cost of $300 or $400 instead of a consulting fee of $1500 to $4000.

Demonstration

A *demonstration* is a method of instruction in which the trainer actually performs an operation, and in doing so shows the trainees how and what to do and through explanations brings out the why, where, and when it ought to be done.

There are some problems in the demonstration method:

It requires a trainer who is highly skilled in the material to be demonstrated.

It requires special classroom arrangement, equipment, and aids.

Other than giving the trainees an overview of the process, it often provides little in terms of positive benefits. We have seen situations in which trainees have been negatively motivated after a demonstration. For example, in an interview workshop if the trainer gave a highly skilled demonstration of how an interview ought to be conducted, it is quite possible that the trainees watching this performance will decide, "Wow, there is no way we could ever do it that well."

Although we do not intend to discuss Job Instruction Training (J.I.T.) we do recommend the discussions on demonstration in any good J.I.T. handbook, as they provide an outstanding resource for procedures in demonstration training.

Reading Handouts

A technique that is commonly used to provide content input is reading handouts. Most often these reading handouts are given as an overnight or as a lunchtime assignment. This is particularly true if the reading is more than a few pages. On the other hand, when trainers design training programs to be delivered by nonprofessional training personnel, for example, by line supervisors, the best content input technique is assignment of a precise, well-defined reading that the trainer passes out at an appropriate time and allows time for them to read.

Reading handouts are often too long. The trainer should not try to tell the trainees more than they really need to know. Going back to the training model (Figure 5.1), the prime purpose of the content input portion of the program is to provide the trainees with a model against which they can measure performance and behavior. They do not need to know everything about a subject in order to do this. For example, in one of our communications training programs based upon Transactional Analysis, the entire content input on the parent, adult, and child models is written in less than 2000 words.[5] This gives the participants sufficient information to analyze their communication styles. On the other hand, when we are called upon to deliver a parent-adult-child lecture in person, it is not unusual for us to spend from 45 minutes to one hour delivering the same material.

There are two problems inherent in using reading handouts for delivering content input:

> Not all trainees read at the same rate. Therefore, some will be finished before others. These lapses and slowdowns in the training process could be dysfunctional.
>
> Preparation time is increased when there is a need to write out the content input in precise and brief paragraphs.

Programmed Instruction

Programmed instruction is a method of self-instruction in which the trainees work through carefully sequenced materials in order to arrive at a specific piece of knowledge. The trainees proceed through the program at their own rate and receive immediate feedback on the correctness of their responses before proceeding to the next step.

Programmed instruction often is used as prework in order that all the trainees get to a necessary level of skill or knowledge. It also can be used in a modular design: by using a pretest, the trainer can reduce training time. Those trainees who show through the pretest

---

[5] D. Michalak and R. Olson, *Transactional Analysis on the Job* (Sterling Forest, N.Y.: Xicom, Inc., 1974).

that they need certain modules can work on their own with programmed instruction to learn the material; those who show that they do not need the training can move on without having to sit through an unnecessary class session.

There are some problems in using programmed instruction:

It requires careful and skillful preparation.

It sometimes requires outside commercial help that may be too costly. Unless the number of trainees who will use the program is sufficient, the increased costs may not be justifiable.

It requires considerable lead time.

OTHER FACTORS TO CONSIDER
IN DESIGNING TRAINING PROGRAMS

Teaching versus Learning

"If the student hasn't learned, the teacher hasn't taught" is an old adage in education circles. It points out that there is, in fact, an essential difference between teaching and learning. In the teaching model someone who is supposedly knowledgeable on a subject stands in front of a group and transmits that knowledge through lecture and demonstration. The teacher's job is to talk and the student's job is to listen. Unfortunately, this is an inefficient model because the students may finish their job earlier than the teacher finishes his or hers. Also, in the teaching model the responsibility for transmitting the knowledge from the teacher to the students lies with the teacher. It is the teacher's job to present the material well, to select good films that can get the intended message across to the students, and to select clear communication and visual aids. These are the touchstones of the teaching model.

The Learning Model

The learning model differs from the teaching model. The responsibility for the learning is shared by the teacher and the student. In many learning model situations, the term "teacher" is not used because of its connotation of the "seat of wisdom." Instead, the teacher is referred to as a "facilitator" or a "catalyst," and the trainees are referred to as "participants" or "learners" rather than "students."

Another essential feature of the learning model is that the method chosen for teaching is one that can best help the students learn what they need to learn and meet the behavioral objectives rather than one that the teacher likes best and feels most comfortable with.

Participation

The more the learners participate in the training, the greater will be its effectiveness and the more likely will the learners internalize the concepts under consideration. Those who teach management skills spend a good deal of time discussing and even using exercises or experiments to demonstrate the value of involvement. If managers involve their people in decision making, their people will be more committed to a decision and more likely to implement it in ensuing months. These same principles hold true in training. Adult trainees particularly need to be involved in objective setting, a choice of activities, and the evaluation. This can be done in the needs analysis, in the prework, or in the various segments of the program.

Meaningfulness of Content

The more meaningful the subject matter is to the trainees, the more they will be able to learn it. In order to make the content as meaningful to the trainees as possible, the program should be designed so that content inputs, examples, practice sessions, and feedback relate to their experiences, interests, and values or to their recognized immediate future activities. As an example, in a training program for aspiring supervisors, the material will be more meaningful to the trainees if they are told, and have some reason to believe, that the content is material that they will use when they become supervisors.

A word about examples used in training programs is necessary here. A common complaint from trainers is that the participants have a difficult time transferring the information received from examples or films if the situations demonstrated are not from their own field. For this reason, trainers ought to have available a store of examples relevant to the participants' work situations. On the other hand, a trainer may have a film that really demonstrates a specific piece of information better than could be done by talking about it, but the film is not related to the participants' work situations. For example, a trainer may use a film that is an excellent example of body language in a sales situation; the trainees are expected to learn how to recognize certain body language. The action in the film happens to take place in a drugstore. The trainer spends some time setting the stage. Before showing the film, he or she says such things as, "Ignore the fact that the scene is taking place in a drugstore and just look at what is happening. Look at the underlying principles. Look at the people, because the very kinds of body language that you see in this film, happen on your jobs." By preparing the participants this way, the trainer can help them get past the "turn-off" hurdle if the film does not fit their area of perceived meaningfulness.

Entrance Level of Trainees

The level or the type of present knowledge that the trainees have is one of the most important factors for trainers to consider in determining whether or not the learning in the classroom will happen. Sometimes the trainees' attitudes or beliefs strongly influence their current ability to learn new ideas. New concepts are more easily accepted if they do not interfere with earlier learned behaviors and experiences, for we frequently are "frozen" into our previous learning experiences and often reject new ideas that contradict previous experiences. This problem can be overcome if the trainer presents an "unfreezing" experience early in the training, for example, a pretest. In a course on communications, if an exercise is videotaped and the trainees are allowed to see how they have communicated and are allowed to recognize their deficiencies in communicating, the likelihood that the trainees will be motivated to learn increases.

Selective Perception

Selective perception is a phenomenon that trainers discuss in their management skills and communications workshops. The concept refers to a tendency that people have to hear what they want to hear and to screen out other information. Managers are taught that just because they say something to their employees does not mean that their employees will see it that way. The only way to deal with this problem is to keep the lines of communication open at all times. Continued discussions will eventually force misconceptions, contradictory information, or partially accurate information to surface.

The Whole versus the Part

There are certain types of learning—problem solving, for example— in which the trainees are more likely to learn if they are presented with the complete model to be learned rather than one step at a time. This allows them to recognize the "why's" of the various steps and substeps when they are presented with them later.

When presenting the overall model, the trainer should present the strategy or the plan of attack beforehand and tell the trainees what they are going to see. Then the trainer can point out and label each of the steps as it is introduced. The reason why each step is necessary, the results of each step, what would happen if the step were omitted can be pointed out. In this way, the trainees will understand the overall model and will not be lost in the middle of the training program, wondering how various parts fit into the whole.

Practice

The old rule that practice makes perfect is not necessarily true. Let us revise it to read, "Practice with feedback makes perfect." The trouble with just practice can easily be demonstrated if we look at typical golfers. They practice a good deal, but they are not getting correct feedback from an expert golfer.

As we noted earlier, the practice sessions in the classroom ought to be as job specific as possible. It is more effective if the trainer spaces the practice sessions over a period of time or at regular intervals rather than all at one time. As the training program continues, the difficulty of the practice session demands should increase. The first role-playing used ought to be easier to handle than the second.

In some practice situations, it is an excellent idea for the trainer to make the situation tougher than the one the trainees will have to face on the job. One way the trainer can do this is by having supervisors act as the foils in the role-playing situation. Because the supervisors know all the "in's" and "out's" of the real-life situation, they can be tougher opponents in role-playing than the other trainees with each other. In this way the transfer from the classroom to the job often happens more easily.

Job Aids in Practice Sessions

In the early practice sessions, it may be advisable for the trainer to use job aids to prompt the trainees. These jobs aids can be pictures, memory devices, checklists, flow charts, and so on. As the practice sessions continue and as the learning progresses, these job aids can be gradually withdrawn.

If the class is working on a problem analysis situation, the first time the trainees go through the problem analysis they probably should have a diagram as a reference, which shows them the steps to take in conducting the problem analysis. The second time they can try doing the analysis without looking (or looking as little as possible) at the diagram. And the third time, they should try to do it without using the diagram at all. Obviously, if the diagram is very complex, rather than train them in the process the trainer may want to train them on how to use the diagram. The principle here is that the job aids should be withdrawn gradually, and this can happen either naturally or by design.

Novelty

In designing a program, trainers should recognize that there are times when novelty for the sake of novelty is appropriate. This means using a variety of content inputs. This may seem to be axiomatic, but it is a fact that too many trainers overlook. The attention span of an interested adult is a maximum of 20 minutes. This means that if a trainer lectures for an hour, he or she is going to lose them at least three times and probably more often than that; of course, it is possible the trainer may lose them only once—one-third of the way into the lecture.

If the content input is going to last for an hour, there are a number of things that can be done to produce novelty in order to stimulate attention. If slides are being shown, for example, a simple technique like changing the color of the slides helps; if a lecture is being given, an obvious change-of-pace technique like pausing at various points in the lecture to stimulate discussion about a point just covered helps.

Team teaching often keeps the trainees from getting bored because of the change from one trainer to another.

Need to Know versus Nice to Know

Learning is facilitated if only the essential subject matter is presented. Trainers sometimes try to teach everything that is known about a specific subject when it is not necessary. This leads to a discussion of something that we have already talked about, that is, the difference between education and training. In most educational situations, the objective for the student is to learn the concepts. In training situations, learning the concepts is an intermediate step toward applying the concepts. A term that fits here is "need to know" as opposed to "nice to know." There are many concepts that are nice to know in a job situation, but for the trainees to use the information on the job, the trainer ought to deal only with the "need to know." A good deal of time, effort, and money can be saved in this way.

Sequencing

In determining the sequence of events while designing a training program, trainers must refer to their behavioral objectives and to the prerequisite skills and knowledge for each of those objectives. The question that trainers need to keep asking themselves is, "What do the trainees need to know or to be able to do in order to participate in this phase of the training?" By asking themselves this question, trainers will find that the sequencing of the training events falls quite naturally into place.

One other rule for sequencing is that the learning ought to progress from the general to the specific, from the known to the unknown. In the early training modules, general concepts ought to be introduced, and only after these concepts have been assimilated and accepted by the trainees, should they move to specific applications.

Prework Assignments

The question of whether or not to include prework assignments in a training design is one that all trainers ought to address. There are a number of advantages to prework assignments. Among them are the following:

Time can be saved in the classroom portion of the training if the trainees complete some part of the work prior to coming to the training program.

The trainees' level of knowledge can be brought to a common minimum level through the use of prereadings.

Feedback instruments that will be scored and evaluated in the training program can be completed while the trainees are still on the job and thus will be a better reflection of the real job situation.

One of the major drawbacks to assigning prework assignments in any training program is that not all of the trainees are able to or choose to complete the prework assignments. There are some organizations, such as public accounting firms, that have designed systems in which the trainees must show proof of having completed at least two-thirds of the prework assignments before they are allowed to enter into a training program. The company's position on this is quite valid. If the firm is spending large sums of money both in terms of actual dollars and in terms of in giving employees time off the job to attend a training program, the company has a right to expect that the employees will make maximum use of this resource, and if, in fact, completing the prework assignments is an important part of the program, the company has a right to insist that they be completed.

A common mistake that trainers make regarding prework assignments is that they do not refer in the training program to the prework completed by the participants. This is particularly unfortunate and can turn off trainees to the program, particularly those who have spent a number of hours working on the prework assignments. The basic rule here is that when the trainer assigns prework, he or she should ask, "What will the trainees get for their efforts and how will their work be tied into the training program?"

Participant Teams

If the purpose of the training program is to have peer pressure influence the training of the participants, it is necessary that a team spirit be developed. In programs in which there will be feedback from the peers to the participants in terms of how the participants have acted during the program and in those situations in which there will be coaching and counseling as a part of the transfer-to-job sequence, the teams should be kept together for the entire program. In workshops in which this is not the case (the peer influence is not going to be a prime source of the learning), the teams should be mixed up daily, either deliberately or randomly, so that the participants will have maximum exposure to other ideas and to other people.

The trainer should avoid including people on the same team who are in direct reporting relationships. There are a number of very practical reasons for this, the first of which is to avoid the undue influence of the person who is perceived to be in greater authority or in a more prestigious position. Also, in a training program there is liable to be a good deal of experimentation; in fact, there ought to be. When a person experiments with new behavior, there is a strong possibility of failure. This is alright because by analyzing this failure, real learning often takes place. However, in a situation in which a boss and a subordinate are in the same group, there are going to be tremendous pressures on both to not look bad in front of the other. This will mean that the two of them may be very low risk-takers in the training situation, and the consequence may be that learning will be minimized.

Sessions should be designed so that trainees sometimes get feedback and content input from their peers. For example, if an in-basket exercise is used, the trainer will find that trainees learn more about organizing, controlling, and delegating if the trainer avoids dictating "rights" and "wrongs" and instead allows them to find out from other participants how items should have been handled.

When we design a program to be participative and interactive, we insist that a maximum of 30 people be included in the program, and, in fact, this may even be a bit too high. Once the group is larger than this, there is some expectation among the trainees that the activity will be leader-centered more than participant-centered.

The trainees should work in subgroups of five or six. One advantage a six-person team has over a five-person team is that six people can further be broken down into two groups of three people or three groups of two people. This increases the flexibility a trainer has in designing a program.

CONCLUSION

In the most obvious sense, the trainer's product is the course or program being conducted. Although the effectiveness of the training program is determined by what is done before and after the training, the trainer's product is usually considered to be the program itself.

The adult learner must be involved in the learning process. Numerous elements of design can be taken into account to assure that learning is occurring, to hold the learner's interest, and to provide real experience in applying concepts.

Additional Reading

1. *Structured Experiences for Human Relations Training*, Vol. 1–7, Pfeiffer, J. W. and Jones, I. E. (Eds.), La Jolla, Calif.: University Associates, 1972 to present.
2. *The Conditions of Learning*, Gagne, R. M., New York: Holt, Rinehart and Winston, 1965.
3. *Handbook of Creative Learning Exercises*, Engel, H. M., Houston: Gulf, 1973.
4. *Affective Education: Strategies for Experiential Learning*, Thayer, L. (Ed.), La Jolla, Calif.: University Associates, 1976.
5. *Guide for Developing Audio-Visual Instructional Materials*, Bell, N. T., Ann Arbor, Mich.: Resources, 1972.

6. *The Guide to Simulation Games for Education and Training,* Zuckerman, D. W. and Horn, R. E., Cambridge, Mass.: Information Resources, 1976.
7. *Instrumentation in Human Relations Training,* Pfeiffer, J. W. and Jones, J. J. (Eds.), La Jolla, Calif.: University Associates, 1973.

Chapter 6
Conducting
Training Programs

Our comments on the subject of conducting training programs will be brief. There are a number of excellent books on the subject, and we do not feel it is necessary to cover the same ground in this chapter. We will discuss those aspects of the classroom portion of training that are particularly pertinent to the entire training process as we have outlined it, and some "tricks of the trade" that we have come across in our years of training.

OVERCOMING ANXIETY

One of the biggest problems most trainers have, no matter how long they have been facing groups, is some amount of initial anxiety. (There is, however, an inverse correlation between the amount of preparation and the length of the anxiety attack.) For those who have some anxiety problems when they are facing a group, two hints may help: breathing and relaxing.

1. *Breathe*. The feeling in the stomach, commonly called "butterflies," is nothing more than a lack of oxygen in the middle region

as the body responds to stress by sending more oxygen to the extremities. Take one or two deep breaths and hold them.

2. *Relax.* Muscle tension is one of the major causes of pain in the body. Learning to relax is a simple process, but it requires practice. Ironic as it may seem, the best muscle relaxer is movement. Many "platform pros" just prior to going out on the stage will literally "shake it out." They will wiggle their bodies and arms and rotate their heads to get a complete movement of their bodies. One prominent public speaker uses this technique to relax. As he approaches the podium, he bends over and picks up a piece of paper, real or imaginary, off the floor. This stooping and reaching action provides him with the movement necessary to relax his muscles.

HYGIENE FACTORS IN TRAINING PROGRAMS

In Frederick Herzberg's "Motivation Hygiene" work theory he uses the term *hygiene* to describe the job environment.[1] He classifies as factors of hygiene company policies and administration, supervision, working conditions, interpersonal relations, salary, status, and security. According to Herzberg, these factors do not motivate people; that is, they do not make people work harder. Instead, these factors keep people from being unhappy and thus, allow them the possibility of being motivated if the job provides the motivating factors, which include potential for growth, interesting work, possibility of advancement, recognition, the use of one's real skills or abilities, and a sense of responsibility.

William K. Grollman, CPA, Ph.D., who is the Director of Professional Development, Seidman & Seidman, has pointed out that the motivation-hygiene theory can be applied to training programs.[2] The motivation portion of the training program is what this book is about—the content and process of the training. Does the program have good objectives? Is it aimed at real needs? Is the delivery effective? Will there be an evaluation?

There are, however, many other factors that affect training programs that are considered to be hygiene factors. These are listed below. If these factors are not kept up to par, the participants will be dissatisfied; however, keeping them up to par does not necessarily ensure a successful training program. The other motivating factors mentioned previously are still needed.

[1] Frederick Herzberg, Bernard Mausner, and Barbara Bloch Snyderman, *The Motivation to Work* (New York: Wiley, 1959).
[2] William K. Grollman, *"Hygiene Factors in Professional Education Programs,"* The Journal of Accountancy, 137, 1 (January 1974): 85–88.

Seating

Should be comfortable, flexible, preferably cloth (not vinyl or plastic). Avoid banquet style stack chairs if you expect learners to sit more than one hour. Be especially careful with groups who normally spend their day walking or standing.

Lighting

Use dual system (so lights can be dimmed but not eliminated for films, overhead projectors, etc.). Avoid glare. Test by shielding eyes with hand (as a sun shield); if the difference is obvious, the glare is too great and will cause fatigue and headaches.

The Room

Avoid sunlight glare, looking into windows, busy wallpaper, or extreme colors. The room should be dead, that is, should not have an echo (carpeting and sound ceiling helps).

Noise

Check for fan noise from heaters and air conditioners. Watch for adjacent noisy rooms or kitchens. Find out who else will be using the facility the day you are there; avoid noisy groups if possible.

Temperature

Have independent temperature control in the room. Be wary of remodeling that may have altered original air flow and may make temperature control impossible when outside heat or cold is extreme.

Free Time/Recreational Facilities

Avoid resort facilities if there will be no time for using them. Be sure transportation is available to evening or dinner spots if the facility is isolated. Stay away from popular night spots unless you plan very light classroom activity. Be sure participants know *in advance* what will be available so that they come prepared.

Timing

Schedule time depending on activities the night before. Generally the following time schedule is ideal:

Opening to break—short, light, easy, motivating learning.

Break to lunch—heavy learning and input (best learning time).

After lunch to break—short, heavy learning and concentrated learning activity.

Break to close—very participative and active learning. (Avoid lectures, films, or reading during this time).

Food

Keep the food light. Most hotels will provide a light lunch. You may have to pay a premium price for it or perhaps a minimum banquet fee, but do it. Do not have too much food served. Avoid serving carbohydrates—they put classes to sleep. Avoid serving any alcohol except in the evenings.

EFFECTIVE PRESENTATION TECHNIQUES

As mentioned earlier, many books have been written about effective presentation techniques, and there is no need to duplicate their messages here. However, here is a collection of "helpful hints" that have been developed through years of conducting workshops and training programs with a wide variety of organizations. They are offered to provide new trainers with some tools to help make presentations more effective.

1. *Give your listeners signals to help them follow your ideas.* In writing, you use signals like paragraphs, headings, italics, lists, indentations, and so on. Do the same thing when you talk. When you have a list of items, emphasize it by counting off the items; for example, "There are five reasons why a supervisor ought to. . . . The first . . . , the second . . . ," and so on.

Use transitional phrases between ideas as a cue to the listeners for what is to come. Some examples of transitions:

"Let's look at the causes of the problem . . . ," as an intro-
duction to a new topic.
"That raises an important question: Why doesn't management . . . ," as a lead in.

2. *Don't start off on the wrong foot.* It is unprofessional to start with an apology, except as good manners require; for example, for lateness. If this is necessary, be convincingly brief. The presentor who starts by saying, "I really don't know why I was asked to speak here today," is courting disaster. People in the audience will be prompted to ask the same question. Don't start with an irrelevant joke or story. Too many presentors turn out to be entertaining, but the audience is left wondering, "What was the message?"

3. *Keep your conclusion short.* Your conclusion should consist of one or two carefully thought-out sentences. Some commonly used techniques for wrapping up a presentation:

summarizing the main points briefly

reemphasizing the reasons why the subject is important to the listeners

suggesting something the listeners can do to put the ideas that have been presented into action.

Avoid an abrupt ending. Don't just walk away without a clear indication that you have finished.

4. *Be alert to your audience.* Watch the body language of the group. "Closed" signals (arms crossed, turning away, fidgiting) usually indicate that there has been some annoying change in the room environment, or that you have failed to answer a question adequately. When you pick up on these negative cues, check them out with the group, and then act accordingly.

5. *Maintain eye contact with the trainees in the program.* For those of you who just can't "look them in the eyes," pick out three or four friendly faces, who seem to indicate that they are following you, and focus on them. You do not need to look at each individual in the group (although that is preferred) as long as you look at each section of trainees.

6. *Vary the speed at which you talk.* Almost everyone has suffered through a presentation by a monotone speaker. Although we are told to vary the tone of our voices, it is a difficult thing to do. A better rule to follow is to vary your speed. When you are making an important point, speak slowly and deliberately. You will find that your voice tone will naturally lower. When you are relating a story as an example of a point you have made, you may speak much more rapidly. Your voice tone rises naturally.

7. *Make sure that everyone in the room can hear.* The basic rule here is to make your voice loud enough so that you can be heard by the person in the last row. Be particularly mindful of the ability of the trainees to hear each other. Often a trainee who is in the front of the room will say something to you, but the comment will not be heard by the people in the back of the room. Either ask the participant to repeat it in a louder voice, or if that is not feasible, you should repeat the question or the comment so that all the trainees can hear it.

8. *Use natural gestures.* Avoid making up gestures to be used in your talk. Do what comes naturally; for example, move toward the group when you want to get them to answer or ask questions. Your gestures should be made from the shoulder, high enough to be seen by the group. Start the gesture before the point is made. Do not use

gestures that are graphic equivalents of the words that you use. For example, if you say, "*I* want *you* to remember *three* things," don't:

point at yourself when you say "I"
point at the audience when you say "you"
hold up three fingers when you say "three."

This is what comedians do when they poke fun at inept public speakers.

9. *Avoid putting your hands near your face.* In addition to the obvious physical aspects of blocking your voice projection, putting your hands near your mouth may have psychological implications. Often, people who lack confidence in what they are saying display this body language. The speaker's insecurity can spill over to the audience to the point where they begin to lose confidence in the speaker.

10. *Use pauses effectively.* People generally need time to think. When you make a particularly important point in your presentation, you should pause. Let your message sink in. When you ask a question, real or rhetorical, pause. Let the group think about their answers for a few seconds. To the inexperienced presentor, ten seconds of silence can feel like ten minutes, but there are times when those ten seconds are essential.

11. *Talk from notes rather than from a script.* When a speaker reads his or her notes to the group, many people in the audience are turned off. ("Why don't you just give me a copy of the talk, I can read it myself.") Speaking from notes tends to appear more spontaneous and natural than reading a script. The audience generally feels more comfortable when the presentor is "talking with" rather than "talking at" them. Be sure your notes are easy to follow. Write in large print or use oversized type. Don't crowd your notes on the page. Leave plenty of space so that you can easily see what's next, no matter how stressed you are feeling. If you are using slides or preprinted charts, they can serve as your notes. Once you know the content well, you can use the slides to help keep your presentation organized.

12. *Eliminate bad habits.* Psychologists have found that we fall into bad habits because we are not aware we are doing them. Thus, the first step in eliminating bad habits is to become aware of what you are doing. An audiotape/videotape or feedback from trusted colleagues can help identify your distracting mannerisms.

A technique that can help you overcome a bad habit is to force yourself into a five-minute inundation. For example, if you are a coin jingler, get a couple of friends together and give them a five-minute presentation, all the while jingling coins in your pocket. After about a minute, you are going to feel silly and will want to stop, but don't. Continue for the full five minutes. What will happen is that the next time you start jingling coins in front of a group, you will immediately become aware of what you are doing, and you will be able to stop.

One warning note: When physical mannerisms are eliminated, especially those which are symptoms of anxiety, they tend to be replaced by other physical mannerisms. If you have eliminated scratching your nose as an unwanted habit, get someone in the audience at your next presentation to give you feedback about what might be replacing it. It might even be a more unwelcome physical mannerism.

13. *Never memorize your presentation.* Use your note cards for reference. You will find that although you don't repeat the same words or phrases each time you give the presentation, the ideas are the same and your choice of words will be free and natural.

14. *Practice.* Rehearse under conditions similar to those under which you will actually work. Consider factors like the size of the room, the lighting, the amplification system, the seating arrangement for the audience, the use of the podium, and whether you will be standing or sitting. Rehearse with your visual aids so that you will be able to handle them easily and naturally. If possible, get some people to listen to your practice session and get feedback from them. If this is impossible, you should use an audiotape recorder so that you can at least listen to your voice. Time your rehearsal and make adjustments if necessary.

EFFECTIVE USE OF AUDIOVISUALS

Trainers should never let "gimmicks" interfere with their presentation. A friend of ours told us about one of his college professors who walked into class one day, stood up on a table, waved his arms, and shouted to the group, "I'm standing up here in order to make a critical point. What I'm going to talk about today is the most important thing we are going to cover in this entire semester." Our friend mentioned that he can close his eyes and see that professor standing and shouting and waving his arms but that he cannot remember anything the professor said.

Audiovisuals fall into the hygiene category; that is, if they are poorly prepared, they can have a significant negative impact on any class. Numerous books and articles have been written on the subject of effective use of audiovisuals. The list of "how to's" that follows is intended to provide the new trainer with a few practical suggestions that we have picked up from our years of conducting workshops and training programs.

A. *General*

No matter which audiovisual techniques you use, there are some general rules that apply.

1. Don't let your audiovisuals interfere with your presentation.

   Don't present the visual aids until you're ready to use them.

   Put them away when you are finished with them.

2. Don't overdo the use of visuals. A picture is worth a thousand words, but 100 pictures may not be worth 100,000 words.

3. Be familiar with your visuals. Rehearse with them to make sure that they are appropriate to the size of the room and that they are in the proper sequence.

4. Test any equipment that you may use. (Murphy's law will get you every time if you don't.)

5. Don't stand between your visuals and the trainees. Stand to one side and use a pointer.

6. Don't pass samples around while you are talking. Show them to the group as a whole, or pass them around after your presentation.

B. *Handouts*

1. Vary your handouts. Use some outline handouts that require the trainees to fill in information. This will stimulate interest and attention.

2. The chart below identifies the most effective time to distribute a handout in a program:

Handout	Prior	During	After
An outline	best	poor	ok
Material essential to discussion	best	ok	poor
A summary	poor	poor	best
Supplementary material	ok	poor	best

3. Don't overdo the volume of handouts. One that makes a specific point is better than five or six that loosely cover a topic.

4. Leave a lot of white space on each page. A crowded looking handout is unappealing.

C. *Overhead Projector and Transparencies*
1. Try to get an overhead projector with a built-in extra bulb.
2. Speak in a louder voice when using a projector. The listener's attention is divided, and in a darkened room more volume is needed to hold their attention.
3. Transparencies can be made easily. Most duplicating machines will produce them. A little creative thinking on your part can provide some high quality overhead slides.
   a. Don't overload your slides. A black and white reproduction of a typewritten page is one of the worst transparencies there is. The only way to make it worse is to fill the page with numbers.
   b. Color can be used to add life to your transparencies. Pieces of colored cellophane can be taped over your transparencies to add variety.
   c. Two-color transparencies can be used to focus trainees' attention on a specified portion of a flowchart, for example. Use a bright color to highlight one section of the slide and a dark color to partially block out the rest.
4. Transparencies of forms are useful to demonstrate how to complete the form. You can write on the acetate sheet with water-based pens.
5. Mount the transparencies in cardboard frames. This protects them and make them easy to handle. You can write notes on the cardboard frame for reference.
6. Acetate transparencies can be overlaid on one another. For example, the first transparency may be a blank worksheet, and the second one may show the entries on the worksheet. A flowchart can be developed in sequence by overlaying several transparencies. The overlays can be taped to the cardboard frame along one side so that they can be flipped on or off the main transparency.
7. Check the legibility of your slides from the back of the room. A rule of thumb to follow is that one-inch lettering is visible at 30 feet, two-inch at 60 feet, and so on. The blank space between lines should be 1½ times the letter height.

8. Use your pencil as a pointer to emphasize detail.
9. Use a sheet of paper to block out one portion of the transparency while revealing the rest.
10. You may wish to distribute handouts of your transparencies so as to reduce the amount of note taking in the group.

D. *Flip Chart*
 1. Write in large letters (3-inch lettering) with a broad-tipped felt pen.
 2. Consider using two flip charts, so that you can develop ideas in tandem. (Or prepare one chart earlier and use the second one for spontaneous comments.)
 3. If appropriate, tear off the sheets and post them around the room. (Use masking tape only, since most other tapes can damage the walls.)
 4. You might write notes for yourself lightly in pencil on the flip chart. They cannot be seen even from the front row. (Don't put all your notes on the first page; when it is flipped over, your notes will be unavailable to you.)
 5. If you prepare the flip charts before the presentation, write on every other page. This way, you can flip a page when you finish, and turn to a blank sheet so that the participants will not see the next chart until you are ready to refer to it.
 6. Use several colors of pens for variety and highlighting.
 7. Make tabs out of masking tape. Tape them to the edges of the charts so that you can easily turn to a preprepared page. (*Note:* Put the tab on the page in front of the one you want to turn to.)
 8. You can tape pieces of paper or cardboard over words on a prepared chart. This allows you to reveal your points one at a time by tearing off the tape.

E. *Tape Recorders—Video and Audio*
 There are a number of excellent programs available on tape; however, our personal prejudice is that the best use of video or audiotape is to give immediate feedback, for example,
 to a person practicing a presentation
 to trainees in a situation simulation
 to a team in a decision-making discussion
 to a class involved in an interpersonal exercise.
 This allows trainees to see themselves as others see them.

F. *Films, 35mm Slides, Filmstrips*

There are many excellent films, filmstrips, programs, and slide and tape programs available commercially.

1. Develop your program objectives first, and then select the film to fit. Just because a film is well done and makes an excellent point doesn't mean it will meet your objectives.

2. If you use a film without having previewed it personally, you deserve whatever happens.

3. You don't have to show the entire film. If a ten-minute segment of a thirty-minute film is all you want, then just show that part.

4. Stopping the film for discussion at some appropriate point (e.g., after the customer challenges the sales person) is an excellent technique. After the discussion, you can view the rest of the film to compare the group's ideas with those of the author.

5. Leave some lights on (e.g., a bank in the rear of the room or recessed border lights). This allows trainees to take notes if they wish.

6. Use "trigger films" to promote participation. A trigger film is a brief slice-of-life sequence that presents a problem to the trainees; for example, "What would you say next to this employee if you were the boss?" The learning comes from the analysis of what the trainees did in reaction to the film, rather than from a message in the film itself.

RED-LIGHT AND GREEN-LIGHT SIGNALS

New trainers often ask about techniques for leading discussions. Without intending to oversimplify the answer, we have found that the words, phrases, and body language trainers use can keep discussions going (green-light signals) or can stop them dead (red-light signals).

Here is a list of green-light signals:

"Good"
"Tell me more."
"What do the rest of you think?"
"Okay, I understand."
"I never thought of that approach."

Nodding head.
"Why do you say that?"
"And what happened as a result?"

Here is a list of red-light signals:

"No!"
"We don't have time for that."
"Let's hold off all comments until the end."
"That's wrong."
"Obviously!"
Walking away from speaker.

Trainers will find that the discussions they lead will be more vigorous if they use green-light signals and avoid red-light signals. It really boils down to using basic communication techniques.

GROUP DYNAMICS

An important factor in training programs is the makeup of the trainees in a group. There are four different kinds of groups that can be put together, and each is appropriate for a different kind of training program.

1. *The stranger group.* A stranger group is one in which none of the trainees knows anyone else in the group. The stranger group should be used when areas of interpersonal skills, particularly sensitive areas, are being explored.

2. *The peer group.* The peer group is a horizontal slice across the organization, for example, all analysts from an engineering department, all first-line supervisors, or all managers. The peer group is most appropriate for a skills training program.

3. *The vertical group.* The vertical group is a group within which there are direct reporting relationships. A manager, all of the supervisors, and all of the employees within a department might be present. The vertical group is most appropriate when the objective of the training program is to apply previously learned skills to real problems in the organization. The most common example of this would be a team-building exercise.

4. *The diagonal group.* The diagonal group contains people from various levels of the same organization, but there are no trainees who have a direct reporting relationship. The advantage of the diagonal group is that input from various levels of the organization can be obtained. Too often peer group sessions deteriorate into complaint sessions because all the input comes from the same level

of the organization. By using the diagonal group, the trainer can avoid this problem.

TEAM TEACHING

We ought to say a word about team teaching, since it is the primary way we work. We often have been asked by trainers what it is that we do or that we have done that makes us work together as well as we do. Unfortunately, we are not quite sure what the answer is. However, we do know that we do not believe in the "dog-and-pony-show" approach; that is, one of us stays for half an hour or one hour and the other of us leaves the room. There are times, of course, when we do this, but we find that we are most effective when both of us are in the room and both of us are providing input to the trainees.

One essential element that is necessary in team teaching is a lack of competitiveness between the two people who are teaching. This requires a great deal of openness and honesty between them. When we work together, for example, and one of us feels that the other has been interrupting or has been taking too much time, we do not repress that feeling. As soon as it is appropriate, the one of us who is feeling impinged upon mentions it to the other.

Trainers should also assiduously avoid trying to score points by showing off how smart they are. This sometimes is difficult when one trainer is making a point and then gives an example to demonstrate the point just made. The other trainer often thinks of another terrific example. The question of whether the second example is really necessary or helpful must be considered from the trainee's point of view. Too often it is a case of, "I've got a great story and let me show off for awhile by telling it." We find that if we try to think from the trainee's point of view, we are able to reduce the amount of "point scoring" we allow into our team-teaching situations. Perhaps most enlightening to both of us has been the way in which trainees respond. We know if we have done these things because we get immediate negative reactions from trainees. It is a constant struggle, but the ultimate effect is very positive.

While one instructor is delivering the *content,* the other instructor ought to focus on the *process;* that is, watching the trainees for reactions and undercurrents. If the process instructor notices some body language indicating that something is wrong, he or she should speak up—"Wait a minute, I think we've got a question here." The process instructor should also pay attention to the content input through the eyes and ears of the trainee. If he or she feels a little lost by the example given by the content instructor, a question should be raised. This gives the trainees a feeling that the instructors are with them, not against them.

Effective team teaching requires a great deal of openness and honesty between the team teachers. There are several issues that have to be discussed regularly to assure that the team will work well together.

> *Who is in charge?* (Someone has to make decisions; e.g., moving to the next topic, dropping a segment when time is tight, etc.) Often seniority or organizational rank determines this. If the two instructors are at the same level, the content person should be in charge. Thus, the leadership may change several times in the program.

> *What should the process person do if the content person appears to leave something out?* The most effective teachers suggest that the process instructor pause for a minute in case the content instructor is approaching the item from a different direction. (There are few things worse than having your partner say something that you were about to say or which gives away the point of a clever story you were starting.) If it becomes apparent that the content person is moving on to a new topic without covering a key point, the process person should raise a question; for example, "Bill, are you going to cover the fourth question now or in the next segment?" This provides a cue to the content instructor without being a put-down. At appropriate (and usually prearranged) points in the program, the process instructor should contribute to the content. This is most easily done by giving an example, and it gives the trainees the feeling of real "team" teaching.

Additional Reading

1. *Workshops,* Davis, L. N., and McCallon, E., Ph.D., Austin, Tex.: Learning Concepts, 1974.
2. *The Role Play Technique,* Maier, N. R. F., Solem, A. R., and Maier, A. A., La Jolla, Calif.: University Associates, 1975.
3. *A-V Instruction: Materials and Methods,* Brown, J. W., Lewis, R. B., and Harcleroad, F. F., New York: McGraw-Hill, 1964.

Chapter 7
Maintenance
of Behavior

Successful training involves two phases: the acquisition of a skill or knowledge and the maintenance of the behavior once the trainee returns to the job.

We will discuss maintenance of behavior in this chapter only because it logically seems to fit here. In reality, however, it appears earlier in the training process. When establishing a maintenance system in an organization, the trainer should begin talking to management immediately after the objectives have been established and accepted by management. Decisions should be made before the training begins on what will occur after the training.

When managers look at on-the-job performance and find that their employees are *not* putting into use newly acquired training skills once they have left the classroom, they have every right to question the value of the training. This has resulted in the reputation of training as "a nice thing to do" when there is extra time or money available or if there is a need to placate the boss temporarily with the old "we're training them, boss" dodge. When, however, the organization's economic belt gets tightened, training is one of the first places the organization cuts back. Trainers find they have no influence in the "real" world or are treated as clerks who handle the paperwork for various company programs. The answer to this problem is that trainers must pay attention to the maintenance of behavior portion of training.

WHAT IS MAINTENANCE OF BEHAVIOR

Maintenance of behavior is anything that keeps an acquired skill or knowledge up to a performance standard. For example, feedback on the quality of one's work or positive consequences for performing at standard will maintain the behavior by providing the trained employee, either through the system or through the supervisors, with some valued rewards. A classic example of this can be seen in learning a foreign language. If we were to ask some people who studied a foreign language if they are still able to use that language, we would find that only those who have had an opportunity and reason to use that language since acquiring the skill are still able to perform up to standard. Those who have had no reason or no valued reward for using the language have long since lost most of the skill or knowledge they acquired.

A RECENT INDUSTRIAL STUDY

We recently completed a major study of maintenance of behavior in an industrial setting. The supervisors of six departments of a manufacturing organization all attended the same supervisory-skills training program. The maintenance that was conducted following the training program was different in each of the six departments, ranging from a very active, positive attempt on the part of a quality control manager to reinforce the behavior of his supervisors to the opposite, very negative approach of an accounting manager who chose not to put any effort into the maintenance portion of the program. The results showed an almost perfect correlation between the quantity and quality of the maintenance of behavior efforts and the results obtained in each department. In those departments where the managers put time and effort into maintaining the behavior learned by their supervisors, the beneficial results of the training program were still in force 6 and 12 months later. In those departments where less attention was given to the maintenance portion of the program, the positive effects of the training had all but disappeared 6 to 12 months later. In the case of the accounting manager who chose to put no effort into the maintenance portion of the program, the situation in his department 12 months after the training program actually worsened.

Results

Some of the conclusions drawn from an analysis of the data in this study and other similar experiences are the following:

1. Anything done by the manager that is perceived by the employees as an indication that the manager is serious about the training program will maintain the behavior of the employees.
2. The quality and quantity of management's commitment to the concepts and practices of maintenance of behavior is a critical factor in the effectiveness of the training efforts. The more visible the involvement of top management is in the follow-up programs, the more positive will be the long-range effect of the training.
3. Maintenance of behavior activities that relate directly to solving the problems identified by the employees as obstacles to their using the skills learned in the training program are those that are most effective in maintaining behavior.
4. Efforts toward maintenance of behavior can and should be made prior to the training program.
5. If there has been a change in managers, continuing a maintenance of behavior program is a difficult process. Unless the new manager actively attempts to maintain the behavior of the employees, the change in management will be seen by the employees as an end to the maintenance of behavior program.
6. Maintenance of behavior activities are not always those that are generally recognized as positive reinforcement activities. One example of this was seen in an office where the manager tightened up the work practices. She let it be known that lunch times, quitting times, starting times, and so on, would be strictly enforced, and she proceeded to make sure that all of her supervisors did indeed tighten up on the work practices. Despite this "hard-line policy," the data indicated that the positive results of the training program were maintained well. Investigation showed that the employees perceived the changes as a signal that "the boss is finally interested in what we are doing."

7. Maintenance of behavior activities once begun must be continued in order for them to be effective.

8. Most of the maintenance of behavior activities can be implemented without assistance from higher level management. The individual managers should be able to act within their own triangle of influence as though they are running their own firms.

Recommendations

As a result of our experience, we make the following recommendations to management:

1. *If managers do not intend to invest any time, energy, or money in a program designed to maintain the skills and knowledge gained by their employees in a given training program, they ought not to invest the time, energy, or money in the training program in the first place.* Although this may appear to be harsh, the conclusions of this study strongly suggest that unless employees have some evidence that their managers are interested in and concerned about their using the acquired skills on the job, there will be a marked decrease in the use of those skills, perhaps to a point that is worse than the original situation that brought about the need for the training.

2. Managers who do something that they expect to help maintain behavior ought to announce this fact to all their employees. If they do not do so, they are taking a risk that the employees will see it as a chance happening. If the employees do notice whatever management has done, they may think "It's about time that somebody did something" without perceiving the activity as being connected in any way to the skills learned at the training program. This risk is unnecessary and ought to be avoided.

3. Whenever possible following a training program for employees, managers should do the following things when they interact with their employees: (a) begin to use the terminology and the concepts used at the training program; (b) phrase questions in terms recognized by the staff as coming from the training program; (c) refuse to accept answers that are not similarly phrased.

4. Efforts aimed at maintenance of behavior should be begun as part of the pretraining activities. Once the intended behavior changes are identified in the needs analysis phase of the training program, management should begin to develop ways to maintain the anticipated behaviors.

5. Because of the importance of maintenance of behavior activities in any program, training aimed at improving managerial performance ought to include subjects such as contingency management, shaping, behavior modification, and positive reinforcement. In the motivation portions of managerial training, trainers ought to include and perhaps even concentrate on the work done by Skinner and McClelland instead of covering the work done by Maslow and Herzberg, as is currently the fashion.

6. The role of the industrial trainer should be that of a catalyst in helping managers to understand what maintenance of behavior is and what managers can do to maintain the behavior of their employees.

TECHNIQUES FOR MAINTAINING BEHAVIOR

As we said earlier, maintenance of behavior is anything that reinforces for the employees, either through the reward system or through supervisors, the need to practice the things learned in the training program. Some maintenance of behavior activities can be built into the training program itself while other maintenance of behavior activities occur outside the training session, that is, when the trainees return to their jobs.

Maintenance of Behavior Within the Training Session

There are many different activities that can be included in a training program as maintenance of behavior activities for the trainees.

1. The simple technique of building in some practice time so that the trainees will have opportunities for successful experiences goes a long way toward helping to assure that the trainees will have the confidence to be able to use the skills once they return to their jobs.

2. The training program should be designed so that it addresses the real problems that the trainees will face. Training programs that are too academic tend to have less built-in maintenance effect when compared to those programs that are seen as practical by the trainees.

3. A very simple exercise that can be used at the end of a training program that increases the probability that the trainees will use the skills learned on the job is to have them answer these three simple questions: (a) "What have I learned about . . .?" (the content

topic goes here—communications, motivation, etc.); (b) "What have I learned about me?"; and (c) "What does this mean in terms of my job?" By having the trainees answer these questions in writing, the trainer forces them to think about if and how they can use the skills learned once they return to their work environment. This awareness is a necessary first step toward their using the skills when they return to their jobs.

4. At the end of our management skills programs we often use the following as a final exercise in the program. The trainees are directed to answer the following questions in writing: (a) "What new thoughts, ideas, or insights, have I learned from this workshop?"; (b) "As a result of these new ideas, what specific thing(s) do I want to do differently on the job?" (Name 1, 2, or 3.); (c) "What things within myself could keep me from doing these things?"; (d) "What things or people could keep me from doing these things (Who else is involved? What obstacles does the "system" present? Are there timing or location considerations?)?"; (e) "What can I do to overcome the obstacles mentioned in questions "c" and "d"?"; (f) "What help do I need from others in order to overcome these obstacles (From whom can I get help? How can I get their help?)?"; and (g) "How will I know that I have succeeded (What results do I anticipate from my new behavior? When can I expect to see these results?)?"

5. Drawing a technique from time management, we have trainees (especially in longer programs) take 5 to 10 minutes at the end of each training segment to record their *A-1 Ideas.* The A-1 concept refers to a technique of prioritizing tasks or activities for A—most important—to B or C—less important. A-1 ideas are extremely important, and also, as indicated by the 1, of immediate priority. These can be particularly interesting or relevant concepts, things they want to do differently on the job, or just personal reflections triggered by the training. By doing this, trainees will remember the highlights of the program rather than looking back to find that all the details have merged into a "gray mass."

6. One effective maintenance activity that can be instituted within the training program is to have the trainees write a letter to themselves outlining how they have benefitted from the program and what changes they anticipate doing when they return to their jobs. Each of these letters should be put into a self-addressed envelope, sealed, and collected by the trainer. At some future point in time (one or two months), the trainer should put these envelopes into the company mail so that the trainees will receive them at a point in

time when their interest in the training program has begun to lag somewhat. Reading their letters, written when their interest and enthusiasm were high, serves as a very positive reinforcement and will often maintain their behavior for a considerable length of time. Trainees should be advised to reread their letters regularly until the changes they intended to bring about have become habitual.

7. One of the best designs for instituting maintenance of behavior is to have the managers and the employees participate jointly in some part of the training program. In this way the managers will understand what it was that the employees were getting from the program. After a certain period of time the managers should be excused from the program, and they should conduct a meeting on their roles in maintaining the behavior of the employees once they return to their jobs. The rest of the meeting becomes a session in which the managers identify specific maintenance of behavior activities that they plan to use on the job.

8. Occasionally, trainees return to their jobs and attempt new behavior only to find that additional training is needed. There are other skills or knowledge that they need that they were not even aware of prior to the training program. In these cases, the availability of additional training becomes a maintaining factor.

9. Following the simple principles outlined in this chapter, trainers may often find that the most effective strategy for change is not to train the employees at all but to train the managers who will do the maintaining. In the majority of nonperformance problems (discussed in detail in Chapter 2), training will not solve the problem because the trainees already know everything that they need to know. The problem lies with the system—the reinforcer—and because of this the managers need the training, not the employees.

Maintenance of Behavior Outside the Classroom

POSITIVE REINFORCEMENT

The single most important factor in maintaining the behavior of trainees once they return to their jobs is whether or not there is any positive reinforcement coming from the managers of the trainees. Positive reinforcement from immediate supervisors is the most powerful maintenance system. Many organizations have found that rather than passing out certificates at the end of the training program, more mileage is gained if after a few days the supervisors give the certificates to their employees along with some discussion of how things have been going since the training program has ended.

FEEDBACK ON PERFORMANCE

Trainees also should receive feedback on their performance after the training program has ended. This is an example of a maintenance system that can and should be initiated prior to the training program. The trainees and their managers can discuss prior to the training program the anticipated objectives of the program. After the training has been completed, they can continue to meet on a regular basis in order to discuss how well the trainees have been performing since returning to their jobs. Obstacles and problems that the trainees have been facing on their jobs can be discussed and solutions can be designed.

REMOVAL OF OBSTACLES

One powerful maintenance of behavior system is the removal of the obstacles that have been identified by the trainees as preventing them from using the skills and knowledge they obtained in the training program. It is important to note that whenever management does remove one of these obstacles, they need to make a very positive, strong statement to that effect so that the employees will not see the change as a chance occurrence. (This, by the way, is one major way to implement programs of change even though management only wants training; that is, the trainees can identify systemic barriers to their performance as the experience part of the training program. The findings are then fed back to management as part of the evaluation process.)

CHANGES IN THE SYSTEM

Sometimes a change in the system is required in order to maintain the behavior. An excellent example of this occurred when a manager of an engineering department sent all of his employees through a problem analysis program. His intention was to have the engineers be able to use this system in analyzing the problems that vendors were having in various vendors' plants that they visited. The manager was aware of the maintenance of behavior concept, and prior to conducting the training program he consulted with the trainer. Between the two of them, they redesigned the reporting form that the engineers used when they made their visits to the vendors' locations. The form was designed so that in order to complete their reports, the engineers had to use the problem analysis system that was taught in the seminar.

An interesting occurrence has been observed subsequent to this event. During the last five years approximately 30 new engineers have been added to this department, and not one of them has been trained in the problem analysis system. Yet, because the form requires them to use the system in answering the questions, every one of them is able now to use the system. This is an example of a situation in which by simple application of a maintenance of behavior activity, the problem was solved and no acquisition of skill was required as a phase in the training program.

PERFORMANCE APPRAISALS

One of the most obvious areas of reinforcement is in the performance appraisal system used in an organization. It is amazing how often an organization will spend a great deal of time and money to train all its supervisors in a particular skill and then completely neglect to refer to the use of that skill on a performance appraisal.

THE BUDDY SYSTEM

A technique used in a number of organizations to maintain behavior once the trainees have returned to the work environment is the establishment of a system whereby two of the trainees meet on a regular basis (once every week or two) to coach and counsel each other. One of the trainees identifies a problem that he or she is having, and together they discuss possible solutions and approaches.

CONCLUSION

Successful training programs should relate to what happens to trainees when they return to their jobs. Studies have shown that there is a relationship between the quality and quantity of maintenance of behavior activities and the continuing effects of training. Activities that are intended to help the trainees transfer their learning from the classroom to the job should be a part of every training program. Also the trainer, in his or her role as a consultant, should work to get management to initiate maintenance of behavior activities on the job.

Additional Reading

1. "Maintenance Systems: The Neglected Half of Behavior Change," in *Managing the Instructional Programming Effort*, Brethower, K., Ann Arbor, Bureau of Industrial Relations, University of Michigan, 1967.
2. *Maintenance of Behavior—The Neglected Half of Training*, Michalak, D. F., Wayne State University, Dissertation, 1975.
3. *Positive Reinforcement and Shaping, Harless*, J. H., Champagne, Ill.: Stipes, 1971.
4. *Reinforcement and Behavior*, Tapp, J. (Ed.), New York: Academic Press, 1969.

Chapter 8
Evaluating the Training Program

Successful training must meet specific objectives. This fact, although it has received lip service from trainers for many years, has seldom received the practical attention it deserves. Typically, trainers put their efforts and money into conducting programs rather than into evaluating them. They respond to management's request for help by implementing training programs, and the success of these programs is determined by looking at the reactions of the trainees or the change in the level of the trainees' knowledge or skill, or both. Trainers report these results to management in the belief that the training is assisting management to meet its goals. (A common method of evaluating the training department's effectiveness is to report the number of hours of class, the number of trainees, the number of classes and topics, or equally questionable criteria. This is like asking a sales representative to report on the number of calls made but not asking the sales representative how much was sold.) Furthermore, upon completion of one training program, there usually is another problem to be attacked (with still another training program). Thus, trainers seldom have the interest or the time to follow up on the original problem to see if the training had any effect on the trainees' jobs.

We have met many trainers who claim that it is impossible to evaluate some training programs, especially programs in the softer skills (e.g., in motivation or communications). We submit that if trainers are not able to evaluate the training program—that is, if the trainers cannot identify the specific behaviors or activities that the trainees will have or do following the training and cannot identify any benefits resulting from the training, then either the training program is not really necessary or the trainers have not done their homework well enough. Even the prestigious, long-term, "key executive" university programs should result in something more than status or education for the trainees.

REASONS FOR EVALUATING TRAINING PROGRAMS

There are many reasons that evaluation of training programs is necessary. The primary reason for evaluation is to see if the training program has accomplished its assigned objectives; that is, to see if the problem that was identified in the first place has disappeared after the training. If the trainer has identified the cause of the problem correctly, has properly diagnosed it as a training problem, and has designed a training program to attack the cause, the problem should be reduced after the training has been completed.

Another reason for evaluating training programs is to identify the strengths and weaknesses of the training activity. The training department ought to be viewed as a contributor to the bottom line. An evaluation can help to determine the contribution of the training process. The success of specific programs conducted by the training department, the effectiveness of various methodologies used in the training program, and the overall value of the training department can be measured through questionnaires and tests administered to the trainees and to the managers in the organization.

Training programs should be evaluated in order that management can determine the cost/value ratio of the training program. By focusing on the costs of the training in terms of time allowed employees off the job and also out-of-pocket expenses spent on the training, and the alternate potential of these expenses, an organization can determine the cost/value ratio of the program. By identifying the costs needed to solve the problems that have been determined by a needs analysis and by comparing them to the values received and improvement gained after the training program, an organization can make a very accurate assessment of the contribution the training department has made to organizational effectiveness, specifically in terms of cost and profit.

Finally, training programs should be evaluated so that trainers can establish a data base that they can use to demonstrate the productivity of their department. This public relations function of the evaluation process should be an important factor to those trainers who need data to justify their programs. We frequently find trainers complaining that their accomplishments are not recognized in the organization. When we investigate these complaints, we find that the trainers have not done any evaluations at all. Our advice to trainers who find themselves in this situation is that they should conduct their programs according to the process we have described in this book and then conduct an evaluation. Once the results are in, they should make sure that management sees them. Just as with needs analysis, data confrontation achieves better results than does personal confrontation; there is no need to tell management how good the training department is if there are data to support this fact.

ACCURACY OF THE EVALUATION

Before we discuss techniques of evaluating training, a brief discussion of common psychological measurement techniques may be helpful. Like training in general, there is no "best" way to evaluate. Evaluation techniques chosen must fit the situation in which they are used. There are, however, three criteria or measures of effectiveness that must be recognized if trainers expect their evaluations to yield accurate data: trainers should strive to plan evaluations that are *valid, reliable,* and *usable.*

VALIDITY

Validity refers to the measurement of a cause-and-effect relationship, or stated another way, the evaluation following a training program should state not only how much the trainees have changed and whether the changes are what were anticipated, but also how much of this change can be attributed to the training program and how much of it can be attributed to other factors. Validity is concerned with isolating the training effects so that the training programs can be evaluated objectively.

Threats to Internal Validity

Internal validity is the basic minimum standard without which a training program's results are not interpretable. The accuracy of an evaluation can be threatened by the following factors.

HISTORY

Training programs take place in an environment, and this environment changes. Crucial events, other than the training program itself, can account for the change in the behavior of the trainees. For example, a plant manager may have issued a warning that anyone not wearing safety glasses on the job will be severely reprimanded. If this warning coincides with a safety program conducted by the training department, it would be necessary to identify how much of the behavior change is due to the excellent training and how much of it is due to the plant manager's edict.

MATURATION

Often an employee's performance improves simply because he or she is on the job longer. Normal physical and psychological growth needs to be identified and separated from the results of the training program. This is especially critical with regard to a new employee.

TESTING

One of the axioms of testing is that the test always changes the person being tested. In other words, when a person knows that he or she is being tested, the person acts differently. Thus, the evaluation, in and of itself, produces some amount of behavior change in the person being evaluated. The effect of this testing needs to be isolated from the overall effects of the training program.

METHODOLOGY

If evaluation measures or evaluation personnel are changed during the training program, an illusion of effect may be produced. If one observer has different feelings or a different approach to the subject being evaluated, it is possible that the results he or she obtains would be different from the results obtained by an earlier observer.

REGRESSION

Regression refers to the tendency of very high or very low scores to move toward the average on subsequent tests. A simple example of this would be: if we took 1000 people who had two or more auto accidents during the past year and tested them during the following year, very probably we would find that the average number of accidents for those 1000 people would be closer to the national average on the second testing (implying improved driving ability). In fact, the biased sample gives only the illusion of improvement.

TRAINEE SELECTION

The success or the failure of some training programs results more from the selection criteria than it does from the program itself. For example, if the trainees have all volunteered to attend, the results are more likely to be positive than if the trainees had been forced to attend the training.

MORTALITY

Trainees may drop out of the training program. Because the tendency is for the very best or the very worst to drop out, trainers can anticipate havoc with evaluation data.

Minimizing Threats to Validity

An important note must be made here. For much of the training conducted in business, industry, and government, the evaluation recommendations we are about to make are overkills. When a training program is conducted in a department of 10 people, a simple before and after measure generally will serve the trainer's purpose without excessive regard to the validity of the evaluation. When, however, a trainer is conducting a pilot program (that is, he or she is testing the design of a program that, if successful, will be implemented over a larger population), it is essential that the question of validity be considered seriously.

There are three basic techniques that can be used to increase the validity of a training evaluation:

1. *Control group.* In order to control the evaluation for factors that may have caused a change in behavior even without the training, a *control group* is established. This is especially important if the change will be measured over a long period of time. Many intervening variables (strikes, economics, product changes, advertising, etc.) may destroy the credibility of the evaluation.

The control group technique quite simply measures the same factors being evaluated in the trained employees, except that the measurement takes place on a *matched* group of people who have not been trained.[1] For example, if a new supervisory training program is being tested, the 20 employees who have gone through the pilot program (experimental group) are tested before and after to determine whether or not they are doing any better on the job following the training than they were before the training. The control group in this situation would be another group of 20 employees who had not been trained. These 20 should match the experimental group in terms of age, job experience, education, and other factors that can affect how well they do on the job. The control group is tested at the same time as the experimental group. Differences in the two control group evaluations can be attributed to nontraining factors such as history, maturation, and testing. These differences can be subtracted from the results obtained in the evaluation of the experimental group.

2. *Placebo Training.* In order to identify the effects of the *Hawthorne Effect,* a *placebo group* should be used.[2] The placebo group is one that thinks it has been trained but in reality has not. For example, in the new supervisor training program just described above, we would get 20 supervisors, matched again with the experimental group, and ask them to attend a different program— one that uses different methodologies or even different topics from the training program being evaluated. This placebo training, in fact, is nothing but a "sugar-coated pill."

The before and after measures of the placebo group will indicate how much change is obtained simply because attention is paid to the trainees, and this change can be subtracted from the results obtained from the evaluation of the experimental group. This technique is especially important in situations in which the training is conducted for employee groups who have not normally received training in the past.

3. *Random Sampling.* In order to avoid the most common mistake made by trainers in terms of validity of measurement, it is necessary that the trainees who are chosen to be evaluated should be a representative sample of the total population. For example, if Figure 8.1 were a representation of the experience level of the

---

[1] *Matched* means representing a similar mix of managers, background, geography, economy, and so on. Running a training program in one plant or city and using another plant or city as a control would not stand the test of credible research.

[2] The *Hawthorne Effect,* although lately it has been questioned by some researchers, refers to the change that may occur just through the act of measuring. Apparently, the simple intervention of measurement creates a perception of status or recognition that can affect motivation and, thus, job performance.

first-line supervisors in an organization, the 20 participants chosen for the experimental group, the control group, and the placebo group ought to be broken down according to their years of experience, as shown in the following chart:

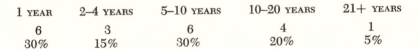

1 YEAR	2–4 YEARS	5–10 YEARS	10–20 YEARS	21+ YEARS
6	3	6	4	1
30%	15%	30%	20%	5%

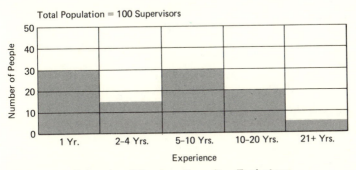

Figure 8.1   Example of Random Sampling Technique

By using a random sample that is representative of the total population, the problem of regression will be avoided.

RELIABILITY

Reliability is the degree to which an evaluative instrument measures accurately or consistently whatever it purports to measure. The common techniques used to assure reliability are:

scores on equivalent forms
scores on matched halves
scores on administrations of the same test.

If a test or evaluative instrument measures what it is designed to measure, it should show the same results each time it is administered. For example, an instrument or test is given to a trainee and the trainee's first score is 85 (on a 100-point test). When the trainee is given the test again (test/retest), the trainee's score is 97. The instrument is not considered reliable. If 100 trainees all received a test and a retest and the difference for 66 percent of them was no more than two points on either side of the mean of all test scores, it is said that one standard deviation equals two points. This is called the *standard error of measurement;* that is, if the test were re-administered a number of times, we would be able to predict the scores within two points of accuracy and, thus, the test would probably be reliable.

Reliability can be enhanced if trainers write the questions for the evaluative instrument unambiguously and then test them to make sure that when various trainees answer the questions, they all understand the question in the same way. Clear and standard instructions tend to reduce errors in measurement and increase reliability.

The measuring instruments should be administered under well-controlled and similar conditions. If the conditions of the evaluation differ, for example, if in one case the trainees are in a room under the watchful eye of the trainer and in another case the trainees are in a room with no trainer present and playful banter is allowed, the results of the two measurements may not be reliable.

In order to increase the reliability of an evaluative instrument, the trainer should pretest the instrument on a number of people by following the rules discussed in Chapter 2 on questionnaires.

USABILITY

The methodology used in an evaluation must not only be valid and reliable but also easily used. The trainer must consider the ease of administering, scoring, and interpreting various evaluation designs before choosing one to assess the impact of training.

Ease of Administering

The money, time, and facilities required to administer the evaluation properly should not be out of proportion to the problem being solved. Time-consuming interviews or overly detailed questionnaires might be inappropriate. The measuring instruments should have clear instructions and should be relatively easy to complete.

Ease of Scoring

If the evaluation's format is not easily measured (as in the case of interviews and observations), the element of judgment is introduced and the scoring can become quite subjective unless specific criteria are established for evaluating.

For example, consider the difference in the following three formats. Which would be easier to score?

1. How would you evaluate the facility?
2. Rate the facility:
   _____Terrible _____Adequate _____Outstanding

3. Using a 10-point scale (1 = Very Poor; 5 = Average; 10 = Very Good), rate the following:

_____Clean rooms _____Service _____Comfort

_____Appropriate for a meeting of this type

_____Food _____Courtesy _____Recreation

Note that in the first sample, the trainer will have to decide how to use such diverse comments as "OK," "Fine," "Excellent," and "Adequate." (Are these the same or are they different?) In the second sample reactions are given but no data are given. It is similar to a typical performance review: If outstanding, why? How can I repeat the outstanding act? If terrible, why? What do I need to change the next time? The third sample is efficient and easy for the trainee to complete and at the same time gives specifics of both reactions and reasons.

Ease of Interpreting

The data must make possible an easy comparison of the trainee's achievement with specific goals and objectives. Graphic displays of score distribution often make data more understandable. If the results are so esoteric that their interpretation requires an expert in statistics, management may be turned off, and the trainer may lose all the effect of the work he or she has done in the evaluation.

FOUR LEVELS OF EVALUATION

Training programs can be evaluated at the following four levels:[3]

Level 1   The trainee reactions
Level 2   The change in trainee learning
Level 3   Behavior change on the job
Level 4   The results to the organization.

Trainers generally conduct evaluations at only the first two levels. They identify the reaction of the trainees to the training program, the speaker, or the facilities. Sometimes the amount of learning the trainees obtained in the program is measured through some kind of testing. We seldom find evaluations conducted at the third or the fourth levels, because it takes time, effort, and money to conduct evaluations at these levels, and trainers are either too busy or too shortsighted to see the value of this investment.

Now let us consider each of the levels of evaluation separately.

[3] Donald L. Kirkpatrick (Ed.), *Evaluating Training Programs* (Madison, Wis.: American Society for Training and Development, 1975), pp. 1–18.

Level 1: Evaluating Trainee Reactions

We call this evaluation "love letters," because unless the training program is really terrible, trainees tend to give favorable reactions at the end of the program. Reaction questionnaires are highly biased by the last half-hour of a program. Any trainer who is skilled will end a program with a "grabber," that is, a good exercise or story that predictably influences ratings toward the high side. We are not saying that reaction questionnaires are not useful. As a matter of fact, we think they are essential. However, the advantages and limitations of reaction questionnaires must be recognized.

Reaction questionnaires will give trainers some important information, which can be used to improve the training program. Questions relating to the quality of the instruction, the quality of the instructor, the facilities, the parts of the program that are relevant to jobs and the parts that are not, the value of the prework assignments, and so on, can give the trainer important information. The hygienic and motivational factors also can be measured here. Often a program with excellent content fails because the surroundings, the reasons for attendance, the political climate, work pressures, or the facilities work against the program.

One technique that trainers often use to get a more useful evaluation of trainee reaction is to send out a second reaction questionnaire one or two months after the training program is ended. In this situation the trainees have had some time on the job and are able to give their reactions to the training program as they relate to their experiences in the real world.

Level 2: Evaluating Trainee Learning

The objectives for which the program was designed should form the basis for a test of the changes in the learning or skills of the trainees that have resulted from the training program. For example, if one of the objectives was that the trainees, "given a bar of stock, will be able to put it on a lathe and cut it down to a 1-inch round, plus or minus 0.005 inches," the test would involve giving the trainees a lathe, a bar of stock, and instructions to cut it down to a 1-inch round with the tolerance indicated.

Testing the trainees at the end of the training program is one of the most common features of academic classes, but in our opinion the testing used in most academic classes is not appropriate to trainers. We feel strongly that except in those skill areas in which the trainees must demonstrate a proficiency in a skill in order to qualify for a job, the testing that takes place ought to be for the benefit of the trainees rather than an evaluation of the trainees by the trainer. The reasons that testing should be done at the end of a training program are

1. to find out whether the trainer has done the job as well as it should have been done
2. to determine whether the design of the training program has brought about the learning that was anticipated
3. to feed back information to the trainees so that they will know how much they have learned.

Except in those cases in which certification is required, we are against the publishing of individual test results. Occasionally we are asked by managers to evaluate the trainees in our programs in order to help the managers make decisions regarding placement and promotion of the trainees. We always refuse to make these evaluations. We feel very strongly that it would be unfair to do so. In an interpersonal skills training program a safe climate of experimentation must be present. One trainee involved in a problem-solving situation may try something new and may fail terribly. If we were to evaluate that trainee based on his or her behavior in the situation, we might be completely off base. By trying something new and failing at it, the trainee may have learned more than anybody else in the class, particularly those who did not risk trying something new or getting involved in the role-playing. Often the trainee who appears to be the least effective turns out to be the one who has learned the most, and it would be highly inaccurate for a trainer to pass the word on to management that "so-and-so did poorly in the training program."

One word about pretesting and posttesting is necessary here. They are frequently misused. As we discussed previously in the section on validity, just the fact that a pretest is given is going to change the results obtained on the posttest, particularly if it is the same test. We do not decry the use of pretests and posttests, but we are concerned that too often trainers think that because the trainees received a 37 score on the pretest and an 87 score on the posttest, they have done an outstanding job. This is not necessarily the case, based simply on these data.

Level 3: Evaluating Behavior Change on the Job

Evaluations about what the participants are doing differently on the job should be unobtrusive. For example, the trainees have been taught to use a certain procedure when they are repairing a piece of equipment, and after the training, the trainer observes them to evaluate how they are repairing that piece of equipment. The odds are very strong that the trainees, knowing that they are being evaluated, will use the technique that they have been taught in the training program. The test *really occurs* when the trainer is not there watching them. Unobtrusive measures are those that take place when the trainees do not know that they are being evaluated. For example, an unobtrusive measure of the value of this book might be this: If we looked into your files and checked the information on the three training programs you conducted prior to reading this book and also the three training programs you conducted immediately after reading this book, we would hope to find that if you had not been conducting needs analyses prior to reading the book, you will have done some kind of needs analysis in the three programs after reading this book. We would expect to see a greater amount of participation built into your design in the three programs conducted after you read this book. We would also expect that some improvements were made in evaluation, design, and so forth.

In order to get an accurate evaluation, a pretraining measurement must be taken. This requires some forethought. Sometimes trainers use interviews after the training has taken place. For example, the supervisor of the trainees is asked questions such as: "What did the trainee do prior to the training program?" "Have you noticed any difference in his or her behavior since the training?" These questions might produce some usable data. Asking the same question of the trainees is an extremely obtrusive measure. The trainee, having gone through the training program, knows what kinds of answers the trainer wants to hear and subconsciously, at least, is going to feed the trainer those answers.

Level 4: Evaluating Results to the Organization

The entire training process was started when, in some way, a problem was brought to light. The question then that needs to be evaluated at the end of the training is "Did this problem go away?" We call this the *so what* question. If the trainees' reactions to the training program were outstanding and if they passed all the tests with flying colors, and now on the job they are using all kinds of new behavior, the question still remains, "So what?" What are the results to the organization? Has profitability improved? Is the organization more effective now as a result of the training? A classic example of how a fourth-level evaluation showed that the training was not effective took place in a bank where a large number of complaints had been received that the tellers were not pleasant or cordial. A training program designed to teach the tellers how to smile and be friendly was conducted. After the training a third-level evaluation was conducted, and it was found that those people who had been through the training program were more courteous and friendly to customers. A fourth-level evaluation identified a surprising and not so pleasant result: the number of accounts being closed was increasing, and the number of complaints being received did not decrease at all. As a matter of fact, the only change that took place was in the type of complaints. Prior to the training, the complaints were that the tellers were not as friendly as they might have been. After the training program, however, the complaints about having to wait in line increased. The result of this training program was of no benefit to the organization: there was no improvement. The training program met one objective but introduced a new problem.

Here again it is essential that the trainer look at hard data and thus be unobtrusive. The predata should be collected prior to the training program in order to reduce the possibility of contamination caused by pulling data after the training program. (Even honest trainers subconsciously want to look good.)

Technically speaking, the process of training should put evaluation as the step immediately following the objectives. Once the objectives of the training program have been determined, the technique for evaluating whether or not the objectives have been met should be designed.

We would like to offer one last thought about evaluation. We strongly recommend that the trainers who conduct the program not be the ones to also conduct the evaluation. If a client calls us in to design and conduct a training program and then asks us to design and conduct the evaluation, we try to talk the client into conducting the evaluation themselves. We will assist them in designing a valid evaluation format, but we want to avoid the possibility of subconsciously affecting the results of the evaluation because of our desire to succeed.

CONCLUSION

Successful training must produce results for the organization and these results must be recognized by management. Despite these good reasons for conducting evaluations, many trainers cannot find the time or money to do them.

Although there is no best way to evaluate, trainers should plan evaluations that are valid, reliable, and usable. In evaluating pilot programs, control groups should be used. Results should be reported to management so that management can identify the training department's contribution to the organization.

Too many trainers evaluate only at the trainee reaction and learning levels. They avoid looking at behavior changes on the job and the results of these changes to the organization. We believe this attitude is self-defeating.

Additional Reading

1. *Evaluating Training Programs*, Kirkpatrick, D. L. (Ed.), Madison, Wis.: American Society for Training and Development, 1975.
2. *Training: Program Development and Evaluation*, Goldstein, I. L., Monterey, Calif.: Brooks/Cole, 1974.
3. *Evaluating Training and Development Systems*, Tracey, W. R., New York: American Management Association, 1968.
4. *Unobtrusive Measures*, Webb, E. J., Campbell, D. T., Schwartz, R. D., and Sechrest, L., Skokie, Ill.: Rand McNally, 1966.

Chapter 9
Other Factors in the Training Process

We have included in this chapter a few items that we have found valuable for trainers to keep in mind and some miscellaneous items that may be helpful. We have detailed an outline for writing a training proposal, techniques for writing leader's guides, and some thoughts on working with consultants.

PREPARING A TRAINING PROPOSAL

When trainers are preparing a training proposal they should try to refer to the items listed below. It is not our intent that each of these items be used in the development of the training proposal, since not all of them will be relevant. But this list of items is as inclusive a list as we have ever seen, and every one of them should be considered for inclusion in the training proposal.

1. Understanding your client's intent or objectives:
   a. what they hope to accomplish
   b. their criteria for success
   c. their measurements for evaluation

2. The behavioral objectives of the training program:
    a. what the trainees will be able to do that they cannot do now
    b. what they will do differently
3. A summary of advantages:
    a. efficiency
    b. cost
    c. sales
    d. attitudes
4. An outline or overview of the program proposed to accomplish the objectives:
    a. format
    b. materials
    c. content
5. Administration of the program:
    a. time element
    b. travel requirements
    c. who will attend
    d. how they will be scheduled
    e. who will conduct
    f. how prework will be accomplished
    g. starting and completion dates
6. Budget requirements:
    a. out-of-pocket costs
    b. travel costs
    c. room and board costs
    d. material and preparation costs
    e. cost of consultant, program design, films, and so on.
    f. any justifications or alternative cost proposals
7. Summary of benefits
8. Statement of actions, authorizations, approvals, or meetings required (assume approval in writing these statements)
9. Consideration of following questions before final proposal:
    a. Who must know about this action?
    b. Who should know it first?
    c. Should they approve it before others are informed?
    d. Will anyone be sensitive to what is going on and how should they be handled?
    e. If the project is due to someone else's failure, how will they be approached or involved?
    f. What could possibly go wrong? Have contingency plans been thought of?

g. Is the proposal decisively presented as a result of the most informed thinking and advice?

h. Has everyone who might have negative ideas with influence enough to reject your proposal been consulted?

LEADER'S GUIDES

It is much easier for trainers to run training programs themselves than to write leader's guides so that another person can conduct the program. Anyone who has written a leader's guide knows that this is the case. We have found that we can conduct a full day's training program simply by following notes scribbled on the back of an envelope. When, however, we have to write the program so that a third party can use what we have written to conduct the program, the need for precision and clarity is increased tremendously. There are a number of excellent leader's guide systems. Figure 9.1 shows an example of one that we have found to be particularly useful. This example is taken from a communications skills workshop.

WORKING WITH OUTSIDE CONSULTANTS

We have hired outside consultants when we were in-house trainers and for the past several years we ourselves have worked as outside consultants for nearly 100 different organizations. We would like to share with our readers a few of our thoughts about the consultant-client relationship.

1. Check out the consultant's references carefully. When you call the references, keep in mind that the only names you have been given are of people who probably will say positive things. Ask behavioral questions of the referrals, for example, "What did the consultant do?" or specifically, "What were the results?" Do your evaluating at the third and fourth levels.

2. Develop your own behavioral objectives. Ask several consultants to make proposals on how they would meet those objectives. Do not hire the consultant unless it is clear that all your objectives will be met. The first meeting with the consultant is often free or, at the most, involves expenses only. If, however, you bring the consultant in several times while you are trying to make a decision on whom to hire, you can expect to be billed at the normal rate.

3. Do not have the consultant who designs and conducts the training do the evaluation. No matter how honest the consultant is,

	PURPOSE	RATIONALE	MATERIALS
Step 1	To present content to trainees so they will be able to interpret scores on the instruments	To increase the probability that trainees will not "psyche out" the questionnaires by holding back concepts on which the instruments are based	Communications Profile Questionnaire Scoring Booklet pp. 1–6
Step 2	To help trainees understand concepts presented	Through testing and small group sessions, trainees will be able to develop more concrete ideas about concepts	Handout 4a
Step 3	To assure that all trainees understand concepts presented	To make sure that none of the teams are on the wrong track	
Step 4	To provide data for analysis		Communications Profile Questionnaire (completed) Two Management Communications Indexes (completed)
Step 5	To show trainees how to analyze data		Communications Profile Questionnaire

Figure 9.1   Example of Leader's Guide

the potential for self-fulfilling prophesy is there. Either do the evaluation yourself or hire a different consultant to do the evaluation.

4. Our bias is that the in-house trainer should not spend much time conducting programs. (This is not a new thought with us. We worked this way when we were company trainers.) If you analyze a problem, develop a training program, and conduct a series of workshops, you have solved just one problem. If, on the other hand, you do the needs analysis and bring in a consultant to develop and conduct the program, you are free to attack another problem immediately.

5. Generally, you get what you pay for. With the exception of college professors who consult on the side and some new consulting firms, consultants tend to charge what may appear to be expensive fees. Keep in mind, however, that when you are quoted $600 as a one-day fee, the consultant does not receive all of it. Most of it

INSTRUCTIONS	TIME
Distribute Communications Profile Questionnaire Scoring and Interpretation Booklet Direct trainees to read pp. 1–6: "The Johari Window: A Model of Communications" "Five Communication Styles" "Commonly Observed Patterns of Communication"	13 minutes
Distribute handout 4a Direct trainees to complete handout 4a When everyone on team has finished, direct them to share their answers	15 minutes
Ask teams to share their best answers to Questions #3 and #4 Discuss disagreements that may arise	5 minutes
Direct trainees to score the Communications Profile Questionnaire, following directions on inside front cover Have trainees follow the same process in scoring the two Management Communications Indexes	10 minutes
Direct trainees to read pp. 7–9 in the Interpretation Booklet	5 minutes

covers the cost of being in business. The balance has to be sufficient to cover the days when the consultant is not working.

Let us conclude this segment on working with consultants with a list of the seven deadly sins of both the consultant and the client that appeared in the July-August, 1977 *Harvard Business Review*.

Consultants' Sins

1. applying tired formulas and book solutions instead of studying the problem with an open mind; adapting the clients' problems to fit their expertise instead of vice versa
2. using a high-powered front man to sell the service and then handing the job over to inexperienced people who are inadequately supervised
3. using the client's name without permission
4. overcommitting themselves because of an emotional inability

to turn down work even if accepting means dangerously overextending themselves

5. privately criticizing and disparaging the client's staff when talking to top executives and criticizing top executives to the staff

6. doing work for a fee that could be done just as well and less expensively by the client's own staff

7. concealing the fact that another company whose products or services they are recommending is giving them a commission or paying them a retainer

Clients' Sins

1. failing to define their requirements clearly and to ask the consultant in effect to find the problem as well as the solution

2. changing their minds and altering their decisions on the basis of casual and ill-informed criticism from colleagues or friends

3. reacting to criticism from superiors by putting all the blame on the consultant, even though they have approved what the consultant is doing

4. not bringing real worries and criticisms out into the open and confronting the consultant with them; terminating the consultant's services without warning or not terminating them when they should

5. interfering and second-guessing on matters that lie within the consultant's expertise and that are outside their own

6. blurring responsibility for the consultant's work, so that all those involved will take the credit if it succeeds and avoid the blame if it fails

7. freeloading, that is, employing a consultant on a small, well-defined project and then trying to obtain free advice on a wide range of other, unrelated problems

Additional Reading

1. *A.S.T.D. Journal*, published monthly by American Society for Training and Development, P.O. Box 5307, Madison, Wis. 53705.

2. *Training*, published monthly by Lakewood Publications, 731 Hennepin Avenue, Minneapolis, Minn. 55403.

Index

Sequencing, 98–99, 101
"Sermon syndrome," 76
Shaping, 123
Shipping department training, 18
Signals to listeners, 108
Situational playing. *See* Role-playing
Size of group, 81–82, 93, 103
Skill/knowledge deficiency, 10–11
Skills needed on jobs, 50, 101
Skinner, B. F., 123
Slides, 100, 113–114, 115
Speaking skills, 108–111
Speech tasks, 52, 85–86
Standard error of measurement, 135–136
Stranger groups, 116
Students, as design factor, 81–82
Supervisors, as instructors, 94–95
Surveys, 26–31, 56–57, 138
Symptoms versus causes, 4, 8
Systemic problems, 17–19, 121, 124, 125, 126–127

Talking speed, 109
Tape recorders, 114
Task analysis, 4, 43–65
    chronological, 59
    elements of, 44–53
    frequency, 60
    how to conduct, 60–63
    of job responsibilities, 59–60
    record form, 44–53, 61–62
    sample procedure for, 63–64
    simplified procedure for, 64
    value of, 64–65
    writing, 45–53, 58–64
Taxonomy for instructional objectives, 70–71
Teaching versus learning, 5, 96–97
Team building, 116
Teams, participant, 81–82, 93, 102–103, 116
Team teaching, 117–118
Technical skills training, 1, 4, 50–51, 58, 59–60, 61, 84–85, 116, 123–124, 138–139
Teller skills training, 140–141
Temperature. *See* Hygiene factors in training programs
Terminal objectives, 69
Termination of job, 14
Testing, 44, 132, 138–139
Testing, as threat to internal validity, 132

Timing, as design factor, 82–83, 107–108
Trainees
    as design factor, 81–82, 116
    entry level skills of, 1–2, 98
    reaction of, 137–138
    in teams, 81–82, 93, 102–103, 116
Trainer, role of, 2–3, 4, 6, 8–9, 28, 39–40, 96–97, 123, 127, 146
Training
    advertising of, 3
    budgets, 144
    as contribution to the bottom line, 130
    cost/value of, 9–10, 20, 64–65, 70, 83, 122, 130, 131, 144
    definition of, 3
    design of, 5, 52–53
    effects of, 131
    evaluation of, 5–6, 20, 44, 119–120, 129–142, 143, 145–146
    as a process, 2, 3–6, 130
    programs, conducting, 105–118
    proposals, 143–145
    reputation of, 2–3, 5–6, 19–20, 44, 64–65, 70, 119–120, 129–131
    responsibility for in organizations, 3
    value/cost of, 9–10, 20, 64–65, 70, 83, 122, 130, 131, 144
Transactional Analysis training, 95
Transfer to job, 5, 44, 80–81, 102, 119–120, 123–124
Transparencies, 113–114
Trigger films, 36, 92, 115
Tryout, 80, 85

Unobtrusive evaluations, 138–141
Usability of evaluation methods, 136–137

Validation methods, 57–58, 61, 62–63
Validity, 131–135
Validity, internal, 132–133
Value/cost of training, 9–10, 20, 64–65, 70, 83, 122, 130, 131, 144
Vertical groups, 116
Videotapes, 114
Visual aids, 111–115
Voice volume, 109, 113

Warehouse skills training, 11–12
Whole versus part, 98–99
Writing behavioral objectives, 71–72
Writing questionnaires, 26–28, 30–31, 136–137